One Man's Journey Toward Enlightenment
108 GEMS ENCOUNTERED ON THE PATH

One Man's Journey Toward Enlightenment

108 Gems Encountered on the Path

ONE MAN'S JOURNEY TOWARD ENLIGHTENMENT
108 Gems Encountered on the Path

The first edition in Korean 2009
Reprints 2012, 2016, 2018
The first edition in English 2019

AUTHOR: Prof. Kyung Hwan Hwang
TRANSLATOR: Nancy Acord [a.k.a. Sohn, Dong Ran]
EDITOR: Mary G. Grant
COVER ART: Rocheon, Dae Kyu Kim
COVER DESIGN: Natalie Friedemann-Weinberg
NARRATOR: Sean Slater
TYPESETTING: Raphaël Freeman MISTD, Renana Typesetting

PUBLISHER: Nibbana Buddhist Education Foundation
12606 Nieman Road Overland Park, KS 66213
www.nbef.education
nbef.book@gmail.com

ISBN: 978-0-578-61704-6

With ignorance, I am the five aggregates[1]
Without ignorance, I am no longer the five aggregates
With ignorance, life and death is my destiny
Without ignorance, life and death is a dream within a dream

---

1 The Five Aggregates: Body and Mind [Feeling, Perception, Mental Formations, Consciousness].

— Foreword —

Upon Reading "108 Gems Encountered on the Path"

UPON READING MUJIN'S[1] COLLECTION OF 108 GEMS, I FELT DEEP respect for his extensive knowledge and profound insight of the suttas.

When he was nine years old he learned from his father, who had a maritime business, that "Anyone who is born, must die." This instructive teaching of his father and the heartfelt teachings of the nobles became a guiding principle of his spiritual practice amidst his turbulent life. Among the gems presented in this book, I was profoundly moved by the following:

> "I do not care about the comings and goings between this and future worlds [lives], but I feel deep regret that the blessings I received are comparable to a great chiliocosm,[2] while the blessings I repay are comparable to a mere brook."

Mujin's meeting with Dr. Sha Chul Kim opened his eyes to the Pāli Suttas of Early Buddhism. Mujin's significant contributions resulted in their eventual publication in Korea. I am very thankful for this fortuitous encounter.

Mujin did not merely put together a collection of excellent aphorisms in this book. He also presented, as a businessman and a member of society, a bold vision of leadership under the heading,

---

1 Mujin is the Buddhist name of Kyung Hwan Hwang.
2 Chiliocosm refers to a collection of many worlds in Buddhism.

"Courageous Leaders and Emasculated Leaders." He encouraged the political leaders of South Korea to uphold the invitation of the Dalai Lama, who is respected by many intellectuals and called the apostle of peace today, to visit Korea. He encouraged them not to dismiss such an opportunity because of diplomatic concerns or minimal perceived value.

Fall, 2009
Taehyun, Jae Seong Cheon, Ph.D.
President of the Korea Pāli Text Society

Recommendation

I FIRST MET CHAIRMAN KYUNG HWAN HWANG IN 1980. AT THAT time, I was giving a lecture on "Yuma gyeong [Vimalakīrti-nird-eśa-Sūtra]" at the Busan Gudohye [meeting of enlightenment seekers]. Chairman Hwang was a curious young man partici-pating in the Dhamma session. Although I learned it later, his understanding of Buddhism was unusual. He possessed the ability to penetrate the core of the teaching. He considered Buddhism to be the final destination of any intellectual pursuit. He believed that one needs to both understand the theory and practice of Buddhism to fully comprehend the Buddha's teaching.

He began to study Buddhism in earnest when he enrolled in graduate school at Dongguk University in Ethics Education. I recall that his research paper – A Study on the Ethical Nature of Silla Buddhism – was about identifying the ideological character of the religious ceremony. Afterward, he devoted himself to the practice of meditation.

The fact that Korean Buddhism's main practice has been Ganhwa Seon must be noted. Buddhist practice is characterized by diversity. Practicing Seon [Zen] Buddhism, chanting [the Buddha's titles], attending meditation retreats, and studying the practices of the bodhisattva, etc. are all means to realize the final goal of Buddhism. Is it right to insist that only one method of practice is acceptable? Might this not be an exercise in exclu-sivity? The Buddha speaks one truth. However, sentient beings comprehend at many different levels. Each sentient being finds meaning appropriate for the level at which he or she exists.

I was the Director of the Korean Institute for Buddhist Studies for 13 years, from 1996 to 2009. Chairman Hwang, who had been a research fellow at the same institute prior to 1996, always provided financial support whenever we needed it, and also gave me invaluable advice. Because of his support, I was able to continue the study of Buddhism.

A few years back, he co-authored with Dr. Sha Chul Kim and published the important book, "Heart Sūtra with Explanatory Notes." Now he is publishing a book, "One man's journey toward enlightenment," which contains his candid thoughts. While carefully reading his manuscript, I marveled at his work. Although this book's shortcoming is a lack of structure, it is remarkable in two aspects.

First, this is a new perspective from Early Buddhism. He quoted Buddha's discourses mainly from the Five Nikāyas – literature closest to the Buddha's authentic voice.

Second, this is a modern interpretation of Buddhist ideology. His effort to interpret scientific knowledge and social issues from a Buddhist perspective is noteworthy. Therefore, this can guide those who are new to Buddhism, while at the same time stimulate new perspectives for those who are familiar with Buddhism.

Chairman Hwang has also reached his twilight years. It is important for all of us to transfer our knowledge to the next generation. The reason why these later years are so beautiful is that they carry all the excitement of the dawn and the passion of the daytime. I hope that he will splendidly transfer his merits of a lifetime – both secular and Buddhist – to future generations.

Fall, 2009
Prof. Byung Jo Jung
Dongguk University
Former Director of the Korean Institute for Buddhist Studies

Recommendation

WHEN I SEE MUJIN, KYUNG HWAN HWANG I SEE BUDDHISM. EVERY-one develops and has a unique personality. Persons A and B are the same in that they both need to take nourishment, and they both need a mate to create offspring. However, they are different because each has his or her personality. For this human world to flourish and be righteous, everyone must nurture and cultivate a unique personality bestowed upon him or her by heaven.

It has been several years since I got to know Mujin. My first impression is still vivid in my mind. He was not a big man, and he didn't have a booming voice. He was thin, with a gentle and quiet demeanor, and unique disposition. That was my first impression of him.

Although many years have passed, he still has the same look that I remember. It is challenging for a layperson to keep the same look over many years. Being able to consistently maintain a wholesome mental attitude toward neighbors over many years is a trait of the nobles. He always has a smile on his face. His smile reminds me of the Buddha's image portrayed in art. At first, I did not know he was a Buddhist. Regardless of time and place, he followed, respected, and served me, a Protestant. He has never once told me, "I am a Buddhist." But after many years of friendship, I came to see the Buddha's image on his face. Even though he has never declared his religion, I realized how much he longed to be a disciple of the Buddha.

He is a polite person. And he is a businessman and a patriot.

Running a business means working for food and survival. A long time ago, our ancestors were farmers and fishermen, living in the foothills, riverbanks, or seashores. I too labor to feed my family and me. It is difficult to understand why people nowadays run around all the time, unlike in the early days of farming; however, the story is the same, then and now. For food, we run, and at times, we crawl.

Mujin is also good at work. Perhaps, in ancient times, he may not have had enough physical strength to hunt or fish. However, in our modern industrial society, one must find food by engaging in a war of brain power. Mujin has an innate ability and talent to win the intense competition of survival to feed many. Through it all, he still has a gentle smile on his face. That is amazing to behold.

Who could love his country more? Although he has not spoken or presented himself publicly, I am keenly aware of Mujin's patriotism and conviction that South Korea will be doomed if it does not adhere to free democratic rules. His devotion and effort in this regard, albeit behind the scenes, is evident. He knows deep down that religion and enterprise could flourish if the constitution of the Republic of Korea [South Korea] is adhered to; therefore, he is a true leader of the patriotic movement.

What is the most charming feature of his face? It is his eyes. His Buddhist name is Mujin, which means "clear, without a blemish." Still, at his age, he has a childlike innocence and purity in his eyes. His eyes behold the true meaning of, "perceiving that the five aggregates are empty in their own-nature" and "form is exactly emptiness, emptiness is exactly form." Hence, his eyes are always clear and bright.

Mujin is a beautiful work of heaven. While I was reading the manuscript of "One man's journey toward enlightenment," I learned a great deal about the true meaning of Buddhism. I am not saying that Mujin is a monk like Ven. Wonhyo or Ven. Uisang or that he possesses the same logic as Kant or Hegel. I am writing this recommendation about a beautiful human being, Mujin,

Kyung Hwan Hwang, who started a small enterprise in Silla's old capital, has done his best all the while trying to follow in the Buddha's footsteps, and is trying to be a Buddha himself. I admire his steadfastness and continuous efforts.

Fall, 2009
Dong Gil Kim
Honorary Prof. of Yonsei University
Chairman of the Pacific Era Committee

— Preface —
Longing to Be a Reinforcement to Free the Fetters of Ignorance

LIFE IS SHORT, IMPERMANENT, AND CONSTANTLY CHANGING. ALL conditioned phenomena arise [come into being] and pass away depending on causes and conditions. Here, nothing is permanent; there is nothing that does not change and that has its own inherent existence.

Therefore, whatever phenomena – the five aggregates, eternal self, individual, and "I" – that exist in the sphere of spacetime cannot be found. This is called the sphere of emptiness.

There are no permanent things, but only constant changes. This vibrating change is both the result and the cause of the change.

I clearly see my state of serious addiction to this splendid ghostly goblin's magic show that we call reality – the sphere of concept originated from my ignorance, which arises and passes away momentarily.

So, I laugh and enjoy. At times, I weep, suffer, and feel sad. If the sphere of concept is the mundane sphere, then the sphere of non-concept is the supramundane sphere. Of course, the mundane and supramundane are concepts created by the mind of sentient beings, and such spheres do not actually exist anywhere.

According to Hwaeom gyeong [Avataṃsaka-Sūtra], if one tried to discard the mundane sphere and look for the supramundane sphere, it would be like looking for a horn on the head of a rabbit. Indeed, I think this is a good analogy. However, this is only understandable to the enlightened ones. For the ordinary sentient beings, it is obvious that the mundane sphere, supramundane sphere, you, and I, have separate existences.

Having shattered the concept of "I" which originated from ignorance, one enters the sphere of truth. If this is so then birth, aging, illness, and death are all a dream within a dream. If I am fettered to the concept of "I" which is originated from ignorance, then I am nothing but a death row inmate being dragged to my execution ground. The Buddha, Gautama, saw the life of ignorant sentient beings to be the manifestation of extreme suffering. He compared sentient beings to death row inmates being dragged to their execution ground.

The reason why we learn and practice Buddhism then became very clear. What is the essence of humanness? What is the world surrounding human life? It is a study of how human beings can be free and peaceful and gain pure happiness. Through the knowledge obtained from such study, one can clearly see the impermanence of this body, perception, mental formations, and the mind which arise and pass away endlessly. One can be liberated from ignorance. One can end the suffering caused by the cycle of rebirth. That would be the first, second, and third reason for the practice.

I remember the teaching by one of the Seon masters: "Although there are thousands, tens of thousands of knots in a commercial fishing net, a fish gets caught only in one of those knots." As an author, the subtitle of this book "108 gems encountered on the path" is a bit too much for me. Nevertheless, even if one were to casually flip through 108 gems in this book – like flipping through old records – maybe one with a karmic connection would be caught like a fish in one knot of the net. If one thing from this book can be a spark of inspiration to free his or her fetters of ignorance, it would be meaningful, in my opinion.

In closing, I wish that those who have listened to the Buddha's teaching are happier tomorrow than today. Furthermore, I hope they will successfully reach the other shore of deliverance·Nibbāna ending the cycle of rebirth by extinguishing the fires of the taints[1].

Fall, 2009
Gyeongju, Namsan, Simwusanbang
Mujin, Kyung Hwan Hwang

---

1 The taints refer to sense pleasures [kāmāsava], becoming [bhavāsava], wrong views [diṭṭhāsava], and ignorance [avijjāsava] in the Abhidhamma [Dhs 195 § 1096}]. The taint of wrong view [diṭṭhāsava] is not included in the suttas. [D33, 1.10 (20), M2, 6, A3:58, S38:8]

— Table of Contents —

Foreword		vii
Recommendations		ix
Preface		xv
Abbreviations		xxv

1.	Be Serene, Be Silent, and Remain Awake	1
2.	Possession and Non-possession	2
3.	Light and Fragrance	4
4.	One Monk's Song of Victory	5
5.	The Five Aggregates' Transient Nature	6
6.	The Reality of the Universe is Emptiness	7
7.	Do Not Be Deceived by "I"	8
8.	Impending Death in the Future	9
9.	Only This Moment	10
10.	Though Flowers Bloomed	11
11.	A Reflection on the Inevitability of Death	12
12.	Do Not Be Self-Indulgent	13
13.	What If I Am Gone	14
14.	The Buddha's Song of Victory	15
15.	The Day When the Sentient Beings' Suffering Ends	18
16.	Busy to Live, Busy to Die	19
17.	What Makes You in Such a Hurry	20
18.	The Venerable Monk I Met in My Early 20s	22
19.	Human Life is But a Single Breath	23
20.	Life Without Regrets	24
21.	Tamp Down Lust and Hatred	26
22.	Saṅgāmaji Sutta	27
23.	Characteristics of Lust, Hatred, and Delusion	29

24. Refrain from Hatred   30
25. The End of the Cycle of Rebirth   32
26. In This Fathom-Long Body   33
27. Enlightened One's Sphere   34
28. A Wholesome Person   35
29. Enlightened One   37
30. Snowflakes on a Burning Pit of Fire   40
31. Where There's a Will, There's a Way.   42
32. My Teacher, Sha Chul Kim Ph.D.   48
33. Addiction   50
34. Nobles of Tibet   51
35. Buddhism is the Science of Enlightenment   52
36. Spacetime and Outside of Spacetime   54
37. Law of Entropy   55
38. Prayer Etched on Emile Bell [Divine Bell of King
    Seongdeok the Great]   56
39. Dhamma   57
40. Common Sublime Principle of Humanity   58
41. The Truth of the Being "I"   60
42. Age is Only a Numerical Concept   62
43. Laozi Says   63
44. An Evening Glow at Simwu Sanbang   64
45. Hafiz, a Persian Saint and Poet   65
46. Realization of Impermanence [an Indomitable
    Mountaineer, Um, Hong Gil]   66
47. Old Testament, the Book of Ecclesiastes   68
48. The Three Marks of Existence   70
49. One Who is Worried about a Potential Loss   72
50. The Verses of Arahant Rāhula and Arahant Ānanda   73
51. The Buddha Renounced the Life-Principle   75
52. Shakespeare's Sonnet 64   77
53. Are All Things Created by the Mind   79
54. The Greatness of Descartes   81
55. The World of the Philosopher Kant   82

56. Heisenberg's Uncertainty Principle — 83
57. With a Hair's Breadth of Difference, the Distance would be like that Between Heaven and Earth — 85
58. Do Not Believe My Words — 87
59. A Mountain is a Mountain, Water is Water — 89
60. Seeing Clearly, There is Nothing to Be Seen — 91
61. For the Fulfillment of the Holy Life — 92
62. What is the Holy Life — 94
63. The Meaning of the Path of Purification — 95
64. Who is a Learned and Wise Disciple — 97
65. Modern Science's Five Methods of Proof — 98
66. The Right Knowledge of Buddhism is an Essential Guide to the Right Practice — 101
67. Who is the Avalokiteśvara Bodhisattva — 104
68. Mahāyāna Buddhism — 106
69. Tantric Buddhism — 110
70. Chinese Buddhism — 112
71. Hīnayāna Buddhism — 115
72. About Southern and Northern Buddhism — 118
73. Ven. Sayadaw U. Jotika — 121
74. The Song of Enlightenment, Gungsukja of Zhèngdào gē — 122
75. Mohammed and Hinduism — 124
76. "I Don't Know" and "I Wish" — 125
77. The Kālāma Sutta — 126
78. The Dhammapada — 127
79. The Saṁyutta Nikāya — 128
80. The Saṁyutta Nikāya, Vedanāsaṁyutta — 129
81. Bhikkhus, Be Dreadful of Gain, Honour, and Praise — 130
82. Korean Movie, "Oldboy" [Sammāvācā] — 133
83. Everlasting Poems that Awaken Me — 136
84. From the Avataṃsaka Sūtra — 138
85. From the Lotus Sūtra — 140
86. The Anapanasati Sutta: Mindfulness of Breathing — 141

87. From the Khuddaka Nikāya [Udāna, Nibbāna Sutta] 142
88. A Single Excellent Night Sutta 143
89. Material Form is Not Yours! 144
90. Truths about Birth, Aging, Illness, and Death 145
91. Dying for One's Country 147
92. Private First Class, Domenico "Nick" DiSalvo's Remains 148
93. The Greatness of George C. Marshall 150
94. The Intellect of President Truman 152
95. Courageous Leaders and Emasculated Leaders 160
96. Mature Ethical Awareness of the Japanese 163
97. Saigō Takamori's Outlook on Life 168
98. Maple Leaves by Thomas Bailey Aldrich 172
99. Four Great Men of England 173
100. Law of Kamma is the Core of Buddhism 175
101. Let It Go 176
102. The Five Aggregates Lack Substantial Self 178
103. About the Path and Dhamma, the Core of Buddhism 180
104. All Conditioned Phenomena are Impermanent – A Hwadu of Great Mystery 186
105. The Mundane and the Supramundane 188
106. Selecting an Appropriate Type of Meditation is Important 191
107. An Apple Tree, A Petri Dish, the Nature of Light, and the Buddha's Quest 193
108. Mujin's Journey as a Buddhist 196

Appendix I: The Illusion of Feeling, the Poison of Stress, Meditation: the Wisdom of Life 197
Appendix II: Path to Deliverance·Nibbāna: the Four Noble Truths and the Noble Eightfold Path 203
Appendix III: Dependent Origination 213
Appendix IV: Charts 219
· Establishment and History of Early Buddhism and Pāli Suttas 220

- Theory of Early Buddhism   222
- Practice of Early Buddhism:
  the 37 Requisites of Enlightenment   223
- The Core Theory of Early Buddhism:
  the Four Noble Truths and the Noble Eightfold Paths   224
- The 12 Links of Dependent Origination:
  the Origin and Cessation of Suffering   227
- The 12 Links of Dependent Origination
  and the Ten Fetters   228
- The Five Aggregates   230
- The Four Groups and 82 Dhammas of Theravāda
  Buddhism   231
- 52 Types of Mental Factors   232
- 28 Types of Materiality   235
- Seven Stages of Purification and Knowledge of
  Vipassanā   236

Appendix V: The True Nature of the Five Aggregates, the
  Four Noble Truths, Torrents of Clinging   237

Epilogue   241
Bibliography   245

Abbreviations

A	Aṅguttara Nikāya
AA	Aṅguttara Nikāya Aṭṭhakathā=Manorathapūraṇī
D	Dīgha Nikāya
DA	Dīgha Nikāya Aṭṭhakathā=Sumaṅgalavilāsnī
Dhp	Dhammapada
Dhs	Dhammasaṅgaṇi
DhsA	Dhammasaṅgaṇi Aṭṭhakathā=Aṭṭhasālinī
ItA	Itivuttaka Aṭṭhakathā
M	Majjhima Nikāya
MA	Majjhima Nikāya Aṭṭhakathā
MAṬ	Majjhima Nikāya Aṭṭhakathā Ṭīkā
NIV	New International Version of the Bible
NRSV	New Revised Standard Version Bible
PED	Pāli-English Dictionary [PTS]
Pm	Paramatthamañjūsā=Visuddhimagga Mahāṭīkā
Ps	Paṭisambhidāmagga
PsA	Paṭisambhidāmagga Aṭṭakathā
PTS	Pāli Text Society
S	Saṁyutta Nikāya
SA	Saṁyutta Nikāya Aṭṭhakathā=Sāratthappakāsinī
Sk	Sanskrit
Sn	Suttanipāta
Thag	Theragāthā
ThagA	Theragāthā Aṭṭhakathā
Thig	Therigāthā
Ud	Udāna
UdA	Udāna Aṭṭhakathā
Vbh	Vibhaṅga
Vin	Vinaya Piṭaka
Vis	Visuddhimagga

— I —

Be Serene, Be Silent, and Remain Awake

I KEEP THIS PHRASE DEEP IN MY HEART AS MY GUIDING PRINCIPLE.

Absence of sound is not serenity,
Presence of sound is not an absence of serenity.
In being serene to achieve serenity,
One is already out of the sphere of serenity.

Absence of talking is not silence,
Presence of talking is not an absence of silence.
True silence does not rely on
Absence or presence of talking.

Open eyes are not wakefulness,
Closed eyes are not sleepfulness.
Right wakefulness does not require
Open or closed eyes.[1]

---

1 Mujin.

— 2 —

Possession and Non-possession

Frankly, it may be that
What you own may actually own you.
Indeed, do not own anything.
Although gold dust may be precious,
Even a tiny bit would be a thorn in your eyes.
I longed to be free of possessions.
Owning or not owning has nothing
To do with non-possession.
True Non-possession is not being
Owned by what you own.
That is true non-possession.[2]

"Appropriate possession gives humans freedom.
But excess makes possession the master,
And the owner the slave."[3]

"We practice to learn how to let go,
Not how to increase our holding on to things.
Enlightenment appears when you stop wanting anything."[4]

Suppose there is a mountain made out of solid gold. Doubling that amount of gold would not satisfy even one human. The

---

2 Mujin.
3 Nietzsche [1844–1900, philosopher and poet].
4 Ven. Ajahn Chah.

Buddha called this the "tainted consciousness of foolish sentient beings."

What is the difference between desire [chanda] and lust [lobha, rāga]?

Desire is the state of mind in which one channels latent energy to accomplish certain objectives. However, excess desire results in lust. Once desire has morphed into lust, one craves [taṇhā] the desired object and becomes a hostage of such object. In other words, craving leads one to bondage, which in turn drags one to addiction. This line of thinking clarifies the difference between desire and lust. Therefore, one must always engage in awareness and clear comprehension [mindfulness] through right striving; so that desire does not lean toward lust – the cause and condition of suffering.

— 3 —
Light and Fragrance

A bright face without anger,
The best of bright faces.
A pure fragrance of the mind without hatred,
The best of pure fragrances.

No matter how sweet the fragrance of flowers,
It cannot go against the wind.
But the bright face without anger,
The mind without hatred, can reach
Everywhere against the mighty wind.[5]

---

5 Mujin.

— 4 —
One Monk's Song of Victory

"I do not care about the comings and goings between this and future worlds [lives], but I feel deep regret that blessings I received are comparable to a great chiliocosm, while the blessings I repay are comparable to a mere brook."[6]

Let's suppose that today is the last day of my life. For the past 365 days, a whole year, I have never been interested in enlightenment; I wasted the whole year due to my ignorance. What if I live today as an enlightened being? That would be far more meaningful to me than merely reliving the past 365 days. So, let me strive for mindfulness – awareness [sati] and clear comprehension [sampajañña] – to live this day as if it is the last day of my life.

Once born, like it or not, one must face aging, illness, death, and separation. However, if one can maintain tranquility and equanimity through mindfulness practice in the face of such conditions, wouldn't such a practice be worth studying every second of one's life?

---

6 Anonymous monk.

5

— 5 —
The Five Aggregates' Transient Nature

THE TRANSIENT NATURE OF THE FIVE AGGREGATES IS AS INSUB-stantial as the inner core of a plantain tree, like a drop of water, like haze, like lightning, like an illusion. All glory is like a flower in the grass; grass dries out, and flowers fall; only the Buddha's teaching remains.

> [BUDDHA] "Those bhikkhus, either now or after I am gone, who dwell with themselves as their own island, with themselves as their own refuge, with no other refuge; with the Dhamma as their island, with the Dhamma as their refuge, with no other refuge – it is these bhikkhus who will be for me topmost of those keen on the training."[7]

> Having been Born as a Human...
> Looking back, the only meaningful thing of my life in this world has been knowing the Buddha's teaching [Dhamma]. Through right understanding, familiarizing, following, and practicing the Dhamma, I experienced the most joy and the greatest meaning of my life.

---

7 S47:14, the Ukkacelā Sutta.

— 6 —
The Reality of the
Universe is Emptiness

THE SPHERE OF EMPTINESS IS A SPHERE OF SPACETIME. THERE IS nothing that has intrinsic existence in the sphere of emptiness; there is only the state of constant change. This sphere of vibration is the simultaneous cause and effect of the ever-changing universe. The five aggregates are also subject to this principle.

Therefore, when one perceives and becomes attached to the concept that things – like human nature, the self, Buddha nature, master, and spirit – have intrinsic existence and meaning, one will be very far from knowing the truths of the Buddha's teaching. The core of the Buddha's teaching is that all conditioned phenomena are empty. There is nothing that does not change. All perceived phenomena are but constant changes based on cause and condition.

All conditioned phenomena have the characteristics of impermanence, suffering, and non-self. Seeing this truth is seeing the dhamma.[8] Thus, impermanence, suffering, and non-self are considered the three gateways to liberation.

---

8 In the Early Buddhist discourses, dhamma has multiple meanings and can be classified largely into two categories. First, it can mean the Buddha's teaching. In this case, it is capitalized as Buddha-Dhamma. Second, it can mean all phenomena [sabbe-dhammā]. In this situation, the lower case is used.

— 7 —
Do Not Be Deceived by "I"

I AM A BUNDLE OF THE FIVE AGGREGATES, WHICH IS NOT THE true self. The root cause of suffering is that I mistakenly cling to "I," the non-self.

So, the Buddha said, "Sakkāya is Anatta."

Do not get argumentative about others or the world.
Ultimately, others exist because I exist.
The world is no more or no less than
A byproduct of the creation of my consciousness.
If I do not exist, others do not exist.
And if this is so, where then, is the world?[9]

---

9 Mujin.

− 8 −
Impending Death in the Future

SOMEONE ASKED ME THIS QUESTION: "WHAT ARE YOUR HOPES and plans for the future?" I answered, "What is in my future is death; I live every day thinking that death could arrive tomorrow."

Therefore, I think that for all my remaining days on this earth, my mission will be to relinquish the abhorrent and despicable state of mind – lust, hatred, and delusion. That would give purpose and worth to my life.

> One must always be prepared to bid farewell to life,
> Since death may come without notice,
> Like an uninvited guest.
> Death is an unavoidable natural phenomenon,
> A consequence of birth.
> Be warier of the ignorant and unwholesome mind,
> Than of death.[10]

---

10 Mujin.

— 9 —
Only This Moment

"The happiest, most important,
Most precious day of my life is today.
Yesterday is today's past; tomorrow is today's future.
Therefore, I must live each day as if today is my entire life."[11]

Jesus said not to worry about tomorrow in Matthew 6:34 – "So do not worry about tomorrow, for tomorrow will bring worries of its own. Today's trouble is enough for today."[12] Jesus said to live today fully and do not worry about tomorrow's problems.

Milan Kundera said in his novel, La Lenteur [*Slowness*]: "The source of fear is in the future. One who is liberated from the future and living in the present has nothing to fear."

They who have been immersed in the
Shadow of the past or the illusions of the future,
They who have never lived
Even for a moment in the present,
Slaves to feelings and sentiment,
Running around in a flurry on a stage called the world,
They will disappear at some moment,
Not knowing where they are going.
It is they who must take
The teaching of the Buddha to heart.[13]

---

11 Blue Cliff Record.
12 New Revised Standard Version Bible (NRSV), 1989.
13 Mujin.

— 10 —

Though Flowers Bloomed

The beautiful spring flowers in my garden at home:
Cherry blossoms, tree peonies,
Sweet-smelling daphne, laurel, and azaleas.
After a while, the flowers wither, fall, and dry up.
I am reminded that my body is not
That different from these flowers.[14]

[DEVATĀ] "Time flies by, the nights swiftly pass;
The stages of life successively desert us.
Seeing clearly this danger in death,
One should do deeds of merit that bring happiness.

[BUDDHA] "Time flies by, the nights swiftly pass;
The stages of life successively desert us.
Seeing clearly this danger in death,
A seeker of peace should drop the world's bait."[15]

---

14 Mujin.
15 S1:4, the Time Flies by Sutta.

— II —

A Reflection on the Inevitability of Death

WE NEED TO REFLECT ON THE INEVITABILITY OF DEATH. IN OTHER words, we must think, "All that gives me joy will change, and will surely leave me." Knowing this, we should strive to perform virtuous deeds and know and see the world as it really is.

In the Mahāparinibbāṇa Sutta, the Buddha said, "Bhikkhus, I declare to you – all conditioned things are of a nature to decay – strive on untiringly . . . Let the Dhamma be your island, let the Dhamma be your refuge with no other refuge . . . You should live as islands unto yourselves, being your own refuge, with no one else as your refuge."[16]

The Buddha [Tathāgatha] said, "This is my last dying instruction to you." Then, he took his final Nibbāna.

"Faith is the basis of the path and the mother of virtuous deeds; it raises wholesome Dhammas, cuts the net of doubt, allows an escape from the stream of lust, and shows the path to Nibbāna."[17]

---

16 D16.
17 The Avataṃsaka Sūtra, the Flower Ornament Scripture 12.

— 12 —

Do Not Be Self-Indulgent

"Vigilance is the path to the deathless;
Negligence is the path to death.
The vigilant do not die;
The negligent are as if already dead.

"Knowing this distinction,
Vigilant sages rejoice in vigilance
Delighting in the field of the noble ones."[18]

The Buddha said, "Monks, for this reason those matters which I have discovered and proclaimed should be thoroughly learnt by you, practiced, developed, and cultivated, so that this holy life may endure for a long time, that it may be for the benefit and happiness of the multitude, out of compassion for the world, for the benefit and happiness of devas[19] and humans. And what are those matters … ? They are: the four foundations of mindfulness, the four right efforts, the four bases for spiritual power, the five faculties, the five powers, the seven factors of enlightenment, the Noble Eightfold Path [the 37 requisites of enlightenment]."[20]

---

18 Dhp. 2.21–22.
19 Devas or Devatā refers to divine beings, gods, any superhuman beings or beings regarded to be in certain respects above the human level.
20 D16:3.50, the Great Passing Sutta.

— 13 —
What If I Am Gone

Whether I am here or not,
What difference would it make?
If thirsty, I drink water. If tired, I rest.
Again, a wanderer is running, in a hurry
To reach the end of the never-ending road today.

The frost came, and leaves fall,
The wind blows, the rain falls, and the snow comes down.
Through the wind, rain, and snow,
Again, a wanderer is running, in a hurry
To reach the end of the never-ending road today.[21]

---

21 Mujin.

— 14 —
The Buddha's Song of Victory

"Through many a birth in saṁsāra[22]
Have I wandered in vain,
Seeking the builder of this house (of life).
Repeated birth is indeed suffering!

O house-builder, you are seen!
You will not build this house again.
For your rafters are broken and
Your ridgepole shattered.
My mind has reached the unconditioned;
I have attained the destruction of craving."[23]

In conventional reality, Vipassanā[24] meditation leads to peace of mind and development of wisdom for a happy life; In ultimate reality, it leads to a cessation of transmigration – the endless cycle of rebirth. It acts as a raft, a means of crossing the river so one may go from this side [the mundane], which is full of suffering from birth, aging, illness, and death, to the other side [the supramundane], where there is no suffering from birth, aging, illness, and death. In other words, Vipassanā meditation acts as a beacon of light that guides a boat in the darkness of night.

In the explanation of the 12 links of dependent origination,

---

22 Saṁsāra refers to the cycle of rebirth.
23 Dhp.153–154.
24 Vipassanā or insight meditation is one of the Buddha's meditation methods.

which is the core of the Buddha's teaching, the Buddha explains the forward and reverse order of suffering:

> "With ignorance as condition, volitional [kamma] formations [come to be]; with volitional [kamma] formations as condition, consciousness; with consciousness as condition, name-and-form; with name-and-form as condition, the six sense bases; with the six sense bases as condition, contact; with contact as condition, feeling; with feeling as condition, craving; with craving as condition, clinging; with clinging as condition, becoming; with becoming as condition, birth; with birth as condition, aging-and-death, sorrow, lamentation, pain, displeasure, and despair come to be. Such is the origin of this whole mass of suffering. This, bhikkhus, is called dependent origination.

> "But with the remainderless fading away and cessation of ignorance comes cessation of volitional [kamma] formations; with the cessation of volitional [kamma] formations, cessation of consciousness; with the cessation of consciousness, cessation of name-and-form; with the cessation of name-and-form, cessation of the six sense bases; with the cessation of the six sense bases, cessation of contact; with the cessation of contact, cessation of feeling; with the cessation of feeling, cessation of craving; with the cessation of craving, cessation of clinging; with the cessation of clinging, cessation of existence; with the cessation of existence, cessation of birth; with the cessation of birth, aging-and-death, sorrow, lamentation, pain, displeasure, and despair cease. Such is the cessation of this whole mass of suffering."[25]

The one who generates the craving is the one who forms the clinging and subsequently suffers from it. This person suffers from

---

25 S12:1.

birth, aging, illness, death, sorrow, lamentation, pain, displeasure, and despair. When one is able to [deconstructively] see arising and passing away of the phenomenon[26] with insight [Vipassanā], the true nature of dependent origination is made apparent. Upon knowing and seeing the reality as is, the link of craving is broken. The turning wheel of dependent origination stops. It is at this time that one will realize revulsion, dispassion, and deliverance. This process of stopping the wheel is Vipassanā – the Gautama Buddha's meditation method. The Buddha said, "One who sees dependent origination sees the Dhamma; one who sees the Dhamma sees dependent origination. Dependent origination is the Dhamma itself."[27]

26 'The phenomenon' refers to the five aggregates of materiality and mentality.
27 The Śālistamba Sūtra.

— 15 —
The Day When the Sentient Beings' Suffering Ends

[BUDDHA] "There comes a time, bhikkhus, when the great ocean dries up and evaporates and no longer exists, but still, I say, there is no making an end of suffering for those beings roaming and wandering on hindered by ignorance and fettered by craving.

"There comes a time, bhikkhus, when the great earth burns up and perishes and no longer exists, but still, I say, there is no making an end of suffering for those beings roaming and wandering on hindered by ignorance and fettered by craving."[28]

Laypersons live countless lives with inherited kamma. The Buddha said that kamma is my master, my mother's womb, my descendant, and my family. The volitional [kamma] formations come about through bodily actions, speech, and thought. Craving and ignorance nourish these three volitional [kamma] formations. The purpose of our striving for right understanding, following, and practicing the Buddha's teaching is to cut the fetters of the volitional [kamma] formations and to be liberated from the cycle of rebirth.

---

28 S22:99, the Leash Sutta.

— 16 —
Busy to Live, Busy to Die

NOWADAYS, WHEN I COME ACROSS SOMEONE WHO SEEMS OVERLY busy, I start to feel shaky and uneasy. I just want to share a cup of tea with someone who is so busy about living. In fact, most people are always busy and, in a rush – so it seems, in a rush to death. Indeed, it is difficult to find someone to share a quiet cup of tea.

> Like bubbling porridge in a kettle,
> Like a flickering candle in the wind,
> Your mind wanders around here and there endlessly;
> See your mind clearly with insight![29]

It is imperative in life to control the weak mind wisely. We need to let the mind be under the watchful eye of mindfulness, a gatekeeper, so that unwholesome kamma does not taint the mind.

---

29 Mujin.

— 17 —
What Makes You in Such a Hurry

Friends, do not be in a hurry.
What makes you in a hurry?
If you hurry too much,
you may lose more than you gain.

Sometimes, why not have meaningful conversations
With a neighbor?
Look up at the moon and take time to study its shape.
Is it a full moon or a crescent moon?
Are the clouds passing the moon or
Is the moon passing the clouds?

What about the sounds of
The great orchestration of a summer night,
At a temple in a mountain with the song of a gentle breeze,
The chirping of insects in the pasture,
And the beautiful sound of
The cold wind blowing over the fall ground?

Why are you so eager to be in a hurry
When the final destination is obvious?
Quietly turn your head and close your eyes.
Your mind calms, joy and happiness will come to you.[30]

---

30 Mujin.

Someone said, "A person becomes unhappy due to his or her inability to simply enjoy life, in the same way, one enjoys leisurely boating on a calm river." I completely agree with this statement.

"Pause and let it go, pause and put it down,
Then the iron tree will bloom."[31]

---

31 Blue Cliff Record.

— 18 —
The Venerable Monk I Met in My Early 20s

I WAS IN MY EARLY 20S WHEN I MET VEN. BHIKKHU KYUNG BONG at the Guk-Rak-Am.[32] He was a great contemporary Seon [Zen] master. He said, "In one day, or 24 hours, you can work nine hours, sleep eight hours, play four hours, and still have three hours left. Therefore, you can quietly meditate every day for at least one hour. If one hour is difficult, then sit for 30 minutes. Calm the wandering mind and develop a habit of sitting quietly."

Although he departed this earth long ago, in July 1982, I still remember his kind words and miss his compassionate demeanor. I would like to share one of his poems here:

"Dimmed by the clouds, the moonlight is pale,
Soaked in the dew, the gentle breeze has a faint sweet smell.
Good, this news of truth! Turn your head and look closely."

---

32 Heaven Hermitage.

— 19 —
Human Life is But a Single Breath

AT WHAT MOMENT DOES HUMAN LIFE EXIST? EVEN WITHOUT borrowing a great monk's words, it is clear that human life exists at the moment of the in-breath and out-breath. If I cannot breathe out the in-breath, my life is over, and if I cannot breathe in the out-breath, my life would not continue.

The Ānāpānasati Sutta [the Mindfulness of Breathing Discourse][33] is one of the three Suttas for mindfulness practice. The commentary of the Mahāsaccaka Sutta[34] explains in detail how the Buddha attained liberation: The Buddha realized that the first jhāna – which he obtained through the mindfulness of in-and-out breathing – is the way to liberation.

33 M118.
34 M36.

— 20 —
Life Without Regrets

ALTHOUGH THE MAJORITY OF PEOPLE HAVE LOTS OF REGRETS about the past, they continue to live life in much the same way as they always have. I wonder how many people live without any regrets. Unyielding lust [Lobha, Rāga] causes the entangled vines of regret. For one who accumulates Buddhist merit, there would be no regret at the final moment of life. Einstein, a great theoretical physicist of the 20th century, said, "Insanity is doing the same thing over and over again and expecting different results." Happiness is not a goal of the future but a choice of the present.

The true value and happiness of humans rely not on material possessions but a wholesome mind. If one is truthful, one will not be afraid. Those people who are overly conscious of others, bluff. Sublimate the suffering to blessing. And awake, right now, the infinite possibilities are dormant within you. Treasures will be given to you when you endure the hardship of difficult and painful adversities. It is not a shortcoming to be a little ugly and poor. However, it is a great shortcoming and a true misfortune not to have a wholesome mind.

> "Then he said to them, 'Watch out! Be on your guard against all kinds of greed; life does not consist in an abundance of possessions.'"[35]

---

35 Luke 12:15 NIV.

"Come to me, all you who are weary and burdened, and I will give you rest."[36]

"Then you will know the truth, and the truth will set you free."[37]

When you know the Dhamma, it will make you free. "Then the householder Upāli saw the Dhamma, attained the Dhamma, understood the Dhamma, fathomed the Dhamma; he crossed beyond doubt, did away with perplexity, gained intrepidity, and became independent of others in the Teacher's Dispensation."[38]

---

36 Matthew 11:28 NIV.
37 John 8:32 NIV.
38 M56:18, the Upāli Sutta.

— 21 —

Tamp Down Lust and Hatred

The door to liberation seemed
So close this morning,
But when I tried to walk through,
It became so distant that I could no longer see it.
I clearly saw the door to liberation under my feet,
Then suddenly it was further away
Than the stars in the sky.[39]

The first chapter of the Faithful Mind [Xìnxīn Míng] states,
"The perfect way is not difficult; only the discriminating mind
makes a preference between lust and hatred, guard against it."

I do not need anything since I have enough,
I do not need to discard anything
Since I do not own anything.
Since hills on both sides are serene, and all is well,
Who would know my happiness?[40]

---

39 Mujin.
40 Mujin.

— 22 —

Saṅgāmaji Sutta

"I HAVE HEARD THAT ON ONE OCCASION THE BLESSED ONE WAS staying near Sāvatthi at Jeta's Grove, Anāthapiṇḍika's monastery. And on that occasion Ven. Saṅgāmaji had arrived in Sāvatthi to see the Blessed One. His former wife heard, 'Master Saṅgāmaji, they say, has arrived in Sāvatthi.' Taking her small child, she went to Jeta's Grove. On that occasion, Ven. Saṅgāmaji was sitting at the root of a tree for the day's abiding. His former wife went to him and, on arrival, said to him, 'Look after me, contemplative – [a woman] with a little son.' When this was said, Ven. Saṅgāmaji remained silent. A second time ... A third time, his former wife said to him, 'Look after me, contemplative – [a woman] with a little son.' A third time, Ven. Saṅgāmaji remained silent.

"Then his former wife, taking the baby and leaving him in front of Ven. Saṅgāmaji, went away, saying, 'That's your son, contemplative. Look after him.'

"Then Ven. Saṅgāmaji neither looked at the child nor spoke to him. His wife, after going not far away, was looking back and saw Ven. Saṅgāmaji neither looking at the child nor speaking to him. On seeing this, the thought occurred to her, 'The contemplative doesn't even care about his son.' Returning from there and taking the child, she left.

"The Blessed One – with his divine eye, purified and surpassing the human – saw Ven. Saṅgāmaji's former wife misbehaving in that way.

"Then, on realizing the significance of that, the Blessed One on that occasion exclaimed:

'At her coming,
He didn't delight;
At her leaving,
He didn't grieve.
A victor in battle,
Freed from the tie:
He's what I call
A brahman.'"[41]

---

41 Udāna1.8.

— 23 —
Characteristics of Lust, Hatred, and Delusion

"There is no fire like lust,
No misfortune like hate,
No suffering like the aggregates,
And no happiness higher than peace."[42]

If I pull out the ugly ego [lust, hatred, and delusion] that resembles a coiled serpent [I am, mine, and myself] from my mind, what is left behind will be Nibbāna, the eternal and immortal sphere filled with peace. The Buddha taught us to establish mindfulness of the body, feeling, mind, and mental objects to attain deliverance·Nibbāna.

[JAMBUKHĀDAKA] "Friend Sāriputta, it is said, 'Nibbāna, Nibbāna.' What now is Nibbāna?

[SĀRIPUTTA] "The destruction of lust, the destruction of hatred, the destruction of delusion: this friend, is called Nibbāna."[43]

[BUDDHA] "Bhikkhus, these four establishments of mindfulness, when developed and cultivated, lead to utter revulsion, to dispassion, to cessation, to peace, to direct knowledge, to enlightenment, to Nibbāna."[44]

---

42 Dhp.15.202.
43 S38:1.
44 S47:32.

— 24 —
Refrain from Hatred

"Hate the sin and not the sinner."[45]

Until recently, I could not accept the truth of this quote. However, it became increasingly clear to me that understanding this quote is important for the Buddhist practitioner.

[BUDDHA] "Bhikkhus, even if bandits were to sever you savagely limb by limb with a two-handled saw, he who gave rise to a mind of hate toward them would not be carrying out my teaching."[46]

[SAKKA][47] "Having slain what, does one sleep soundly? Having slain what, does one not sorrow? What is the one thing, O Gotama, whose killing you approve?

[BUDDHA] "Having slain anger, one sleeps soundly; Having slain anger, one does not sorrow;"[48]

When one sees clearly with insight that the poison of hatred arises upon one's own lust, hatred, and delusion as condition, one can then free oneself from the poison of hatred. Therefore, if one reduces lust, hatred, and delusion, one's happiness increases; if

---

45 Mahatma Gandhi.
46 M1:21, the Simile of the Saw Sutta.
47 Sakka is lord of the devas.
48 S11:21, the Having Slain Sutta.

lust, hatred, and delusion increase, one's suffering increases. True happiness is proportional to the freedom of the mind. Suffering is proportional to the restriction of the mind.

— 25 —
The End of the Cycle of Rebirth

[BUDDHA] "The world's end can never be reached
By means of traveling [through the world],
Yet without reaching the world's end
There is no release from suffering.

"Therefore, truly, the world-knower, the wise one,
Gone to the world's end, fulfiller of the holy life,
Having known the world's end,
At peace, longs not for this world or another."[49]

---

49 S2:26, the Rohitassa Sutta.

— 26 —
In This Fathom-Long Body

[BUDDHA] "I say, friend, that by traveling one cannot know, see, or reach that end of the world where one is not born, does not grow old and die, does not pass away and get reborn. Yet I say that without having reached the end of the world there is no making an end of suffering. It is in this fathom-long body endowed with perception and mind that I proclaim 1) the world, 2) the origin of the world, 3) the cessation of the world, and 4) the way leading to the cessation of the world."[50]

"Knowing this body is like foam,
Fully awake to its mirage-like nature,
Cutting off Māra's flowers,
One goes unseen by the King of Death."[51]

---

50 S11:21, the Having Slain Sutta.
51 Dhp. 4.46.

— 27 —
Enlightened One's Sphere

VEN. BHIKKHU SENGZHAO [384–414] OF THE LATER QIN DYNASTY of China said, "In the sphere of the enlightened ones, all phenomena are one, and the universe shares the same root." Likewise, the Indian sage, Kabir [1440–1518] said, "How can I harm myself when all life is my life?"

The Buddha did not teach the Dhamma to explain the origin of life or the beginning of the universe. The purpose of his teaching was to reveal the universal disease of all humanity – suffering [Dukkha] – and to give us the prescription to end the suffering. The Buddha said, "I only explain one thing; the suffering and cessation of suffering."

— 28 —

A Wholesome Person

What is a wholesome person?

[BUDDHA]
"[A wholesome person]
Does no evil bodily actions,
Utters no evil speech,
Has no evil intentions,
Does not make his living by any evil livelihood."[52]

[BUDDHA]
"[A wholesome person]
Avoids taking life,
Taking what is not given,
Sexual misconduct,
Lying speech,
Slander,
Rude speech,
Idle chatter,
Lust,
Ill will,
Wrong view."[53]

---

52 M78.
53 D33:3.3 (3)–(4).

[BUDDHA]
"[A wholesome person]
Practices the four foundations of mindfulness,
The four right efforts
The four bases for spiritual power,
The five faculties,
The five powers
The seven factors of enlightenment,
The noble eightfold path."[54]

Wholesome deeds are easy for the noble
Wholesome deeds are difficult for the villain
Unwholesome deeds are easy for the villain
Unwholesome deeds are impossible for the noble[55]

---

54 D28:3.
55 Mujin.

— 29 —
Enlightened One

THERE ARE NO WORRIES, ANXIETIES, OR FEAR FOR ONE WHO HAS
abandoned clinging to self-view, attachment to moral precepts
and religious ritual, and doubts about the Buddha, Dhamma,
Saṅgha, precepts, dependent origination, etc. Such a person is
called a noble[56] and a liberated one.

> [BUDDHA] "Aggivessana, Ignorance was banished and true
> knowledge arose, darkness was banished and light arose, as
> happens in one who abides diligent, ardent, and resolute.
> But such pleasant feeling that arose in me did not invade my
> mind and remain.
>
> "When my concentrated mind was thus purified, bright,
> unblemished, rid of imperfection, malleable, wieldy, steady,
> and attained to imperturbability, I directed it to knowledge of
> the destruction of the taints. I directly knew it as it actually is:
> 'This is suffering';... 'This is the origin of suffering';... 'This is
> the cessation of suffering';... 'This is the way leading to the
> cessation of suffering';... 'These are the taints';... 'This is the
> origin of the taints';... 'This is the cessation of the taints';...
> 'This is the way leading to the cessation of the taints.'
>
> "When I knew and saw thus, my mind was liberated from the
> taint of sensual desire, from the taint of becoming, from the
> taint of ignorance. When it was liberated there came the

---

56 The stream-enterer.

knowledge: 'It is liberated.' I directly knew: 'Birth is destroyed, the holy life has been lived, what had to be done has been done, there is no more coming to any state of being.'

"This was the third true knowledge attained by me in the last watch of the night."[57]

What is deliverance [vimutti], liberation [vimokkha],[58] and Nibbāna?

Deliverance is most broadly understood as the attainment of the four kinds of fruition [the fruition of stream-entry, once-returning, non-returning, Arahantship] and the state of mind that realizes Nibbāna. One cannot claim "deliverance" unless one realizes, at a minimum, the fruition of stream-entry.

The stream-enterer is a noble one who has abandoned the three fetters of self-view, attachment to rules and ritual, and doubts; the once-returner is a noble one who has not only abandoned the previous three fetters but also weakened the two fetters of sensual lust and ill will. The non-returner is a noble one who has completely abandoned the lower five fetters; the Arahant is a noble one who has abandoned all ten fetters.[59] These four attainments[60] belong to supramundane.

According to the Path of Purification, there are three gateways to liberation. These are impermanence, suffering, and non-self. "When one who has great resolution brings [formations] to mind as impermanent, one acquires the signless liberation. When one who has great tranquility brings [formations] to mind as suffering,

---

57 M 36:41–44, the Mahāsaccaka Sutta.
58 Although deliverance [vimutti] and liberation [vimokkha] are differentiated here, often deliverance, liberation, awakening, and enlightenment are used interchangeably in English translation. Therefore, it is important to know the underlying Pāli word.
59 A7:15.
60 Stream-enterer [Sotāpanna], Once-returner [Sakadāgāmi], Non-returner [Anāgāmi], and Arahant.

he acquires the desireless liberation. When one who has great wisdom brings [formations] to mind as non-self, he acquires the void liberation."[61]

These four nobles have realized Nibbāna [even if only for a moment] – a unique state without lust, hatred, and delusion.[62] Therefore, the realization of Nibbāna is deliverance. Through the practice of the Noble Eightfold Path, one extinguishes the fires of lust, hatred, and delusion.[63]

Although to become a noble one must experience [even if only for a moment] Nibbāna, nobles do not always remain in Nibbāna. When any of these nobles exit the unique state called Nibbāna, they return to ordinary lives. Notably, even though an Arahant has attained the highest state through the destruction of all taints and abandonment of ten fetters, that does not mean the Arahant always stays in Nibbāna.

---

61 Vis.XXI.70.
62 S38:1.
63 S45:20.

— 30 —
Snowflakes on a Burning Pit of Fire

The wind blows the cardboard pavilion,
Waves sweep the sandcastle.
The impermanence of moments,
Arising and passing away,
Tens of thousands of plans,
Are like snowflakes on a burning pit of fire.[64]

The Buddha's teaching that "all things in the world are in a constant state of flux" is the immutable truth. All things, including "I," that exist in the sphere of spacetime are subject to change because they are within the confines of time. For humans, the stage of constant change includes this world – the world of the 18 elements.[65] So, it is logical to conclude that all things or phenomena in this vast universe are only subjects of observation; there is no "I," mine, or myself that I can hold onto. Therefore, those who abandon lust, hatred, and delusion – with the right understanding of impermanence – will arrive at the shore of Nibbāna. However, ignorant sentient beings will endure endless suffering because they are subject to lust, hatred, and delusion. The Buddha said that whatever phenomenon appears before us

---

64 Mujin.
65 The 18 elements consist of the six internal sense bases [eye, ear, nose, tongue, body, and mind], the six external sense bases [visible form, sound, odor, taste, touch, and mental objects], and the six types of consciousness thereof.

is nothing but a phantom – not a subject of attachment but a subject of observation.

"If one sees the world as a bubble,
If one sees it as a mirage,
One won't be seen
By the King of Death."[66]

---

66 Dhp.13.170.

— 31 —
Where There's a Will, There's a Way

EVERYONE HAS TRIALS AND TRIBULATIONS, LARGE AND SMALL, IN life. I, myself, have suffered several near-death experiences and endured numerous unforeseen difficulties.

While attending elementary school, I fell about ten meters from the Ozagyo bridge while riding my bicycle. Even though I could have easily been killed, I miraculously emerged without a scratch!

In 1977, while still in my 20s, I started a maritime oil tanker business. Shortly after I started, a G/T 50-ton oil tanker almost capsized from tornado-like winds and raging waves. I had personally inspected and purchased this ship, which was made out of steel plates in Mokpo city, Jeonnam Province, South Korea. We struggled and fought the strong winds and waves all night, keeping the ship afloat and keeping ourselves alive.

Shortly after this, in the same year, I was jailed for over a year for an alleged connection to an illegal oil spill from the Samchoek Thermoelectric Power Plant in Gangwon Province, South Korea. I was freed after reimbursing 100% of the damages to the Korea Electric Power Corporation. During my imprisonment, my father had passed away, and by the time I came home, our family was left with nothing. We could have become beggars. At that time, I was the eldest of five siblings at home and was responsible for taking care of them all.

When this oil spill accident occurred, I anticipated that I might be in trouble. The establishment had been enjoying prosperous business dealings, and then I, a young man in his 20s, poked my nose in their business. I had not been welcomed. After this case was concluded and transferred by the police department of Gyeongnam Province to the Justice Department, I was shown a document by an executive of the police department. The document contained detailed information submitted by my business competitor.

In 1997, exactly 20 years later, South Korea was mired in the International Monetary Fund [IMF] financial crisis. I did not see it coming and was greatly challenged by this national crisis.

After the conclusion of the Samchoek Thermoelectric Power Plant case, through 20 years of persistence and hard work, I became the owner/operator of a gas and propane refill station. I also had a corporation with approximately 50 employees. The corporation was a small enterprise with about 1 million dollars in equity. It had two stable lines of business: operating an ocean dumpster for industrial waste in the international water near the East Sea of South Korea and operating a coastal oil tanker business which transported oil to local areas in South Korea. The ocean dumpster business was the first of its kind in South Korea, and it was supported by the two-year commissioned study from the Seoul National University Research Institute of Oceanography.

In 1996, one year before the IMF crisis, our company had placed an order to a Japanese company for what was to become our third oil tanker [D/W 3,500 ton]. We put down a 10% deposit with 90% financing, to be paid back in five years. When we signed the purchase contract, the exchange rate was one US dollar to 800 [Korean] won. With the IMF crisis, the exchange rate went to one US dollar to 1,600 [Korean] won. Therefore, our debt for the oil tanker doubled. It was like being struck by lightning. The initial purchase price of the oil tanker was three million US dollars, including expenses.

Around this time, December 1997, I also had an unexpected family issue. Recalling what the elders have said about how catastrophes come in pairs, I began to understand why people commit suicide under challenging circumstances.

This event left me thoroughly exhausted, like a wilted green! My legs were so wobbly that I could not walk for several days. I could not predict what the next day would bring. No matter how many times I searched for solutions to my problems, the answers were not forthcoming.

But, somehow, I had the will to find the answer within me. I pushed my body to hike to the hermitage, Chilbulam, in the Namsan.[67]

The round trip from my house [Shimwu Sanbang] to Chilbulam, Namsan, and back took about two hours. I made this round trip every day for one month. Through this endeavor, I began to think I might be able to solve my problems.

Five years later, in October 2002, I was diagnosed with thyroid cancer during a routine examination at Dongguk University, Gyeongju Hospital. That dreaded disease, the most unwelcome guest – cancer – had come to me.

In November of that year, I had an operation in Cha Hospital in Bundang, Gyeonggi Province. My doctor assured me that the operation had gone very well. However, after one year, the doctor said I needed another operation. He gave me many reasons for the second operation. I did not mind the second operation. It has been six years since then. I only need to have a checkup once a year. My doctor has assured me that I am cured of cancer. I fantasize that the uninvited guest, cancer, must have been an honorable guest.

I am very grateful to two people who were kind to me during my illness. Although he is so busy that he carries two cell phones, Dr. Cha, Kwang Un spent the night before the surgery with me in my hospital room sharing light-hearted conversation. Dr. Cha, Kwang Un is vice chancellor of Jungmun Medical University [currently Cha University]. Another doctor, Dr. Kim, Mun Chan,

---

67 Nam*san*: San is mountain in Korean.

Director of the Health Promotion Center, Ulsan University Hospital, came from Ulsan to visit me in Bundang Cha Hospital in Gyeonggi Province despite his busy schedule. He brought me flowers and gave me comforting words, "Brother, this surgery is a no big deal. So, do not worry about it." These two friends will remain in my memory forever.

I am sure that many more events tested my courage during my 60 years on earth. When I look back, the fact that I am still here seems like a wonderful drama. I am grateful to my family, friends, and neighbors for that.

This said, once we are born, we have to live our lives with unpredictable tomorrows. The Buddha called this unsatisfactory nature of life, suffering [dukkha]. He condensed this suffering into four broad categories – birth, aging, illness, and death – and further into eight categories – union with what is displeasing, separation from what is pleasing, not to get what one wants, and the five aggregates subject to clinging. Dukkha! Who can possibly avoid suffering? But I would define dukkha as a "great contradiction," because through dukkha, there is a path to the sphere of great truths.

In other words, when we accept the existential fact of the four or eight kinds of suffering and clearly see the suffering with insight, we can overcome this suffering through the Four Noble Truths. For two thousand six hundred years, this has been the Buddha's message to humanity.

We can realize the Four Noble Truths through this great contradiction. Life on earth, home to humanity, is suffering; therefore, it is called the "sphere of patience and endurance."[68]

This suffering is not to be avoided, but rather through endurance and persistence, we need to use it to sublimate our consciousness to higher spheres and transform our ignorance to the right view. The Four Noble Truths are the core of the Buddha's teaching that addresses human suffering.

---

68 The sphere of patience and endurance: Sahā-Loka-Dhātu [Sk].

One who knows suffering knows the origin of suffering; one who knows the origin of suffering knows the cessation of suffering; one who knows the cessation of suffering knows the noble eightfold path leading to the cessation of suffering to deliverance·Nibbāna.

It is hard for one to be born as a human being; it is even more difficult to encounter the Dhamma, particularly the authentic [right] Dhamma.

Do not give up easily or get discouraged with trivial problems. Do not expect to achieve goals or obtain things easily. Things of value and meaning are not easy to obtain. Although I did not want to discuss my private life here, I did want to share some of the lessons I learned. We must condition our minds at all times so that we may not lose courage when facing difficulty. As long as we live on this earth, we will run into both trivial and severe problems.

Using a metaphor, I say, "Let us not doubt that God always tempts us. Only those who pass the test will experience the love and grace of God." Such understanding is part of my religious belief and my view of life.

When a crisis is upon us,
Let us not get weak or intimidated.
Leave our outcomes to be.

If it is to happen, it will happen.
If the crisis resolves or disappears,
Be equanimous and keep going.

An equanimous mind has no
Attachment to likes or aversion to dislikes.

Although it may not be easy,
Through persistent practice,
It can be done!

Herein lies a marvelous solution,
Equanimity is the wise and right attitude.[69]

"Having crossed the mountain and the water,
I thought there is no longer a path.
Yet, I found a village with lush willow trees
And flowers in full bloom."[70]

---

69 Mujin.
70 Yusan Suhchon: Authored by Yuk Yu [1125–1210].

— 32 —
My Teacher, Sha Chul Kim, Ph.D.

THE GREATEST BLESSING OF HUMAN LIFE IS AN ENCOUNTER WITH a good teacher. In 1995, I was fortunate to meet a great teacher. Meeting my teacher, Edward Kim, Ph.D., was a blessing and an honor. Edward Kim, Ph.D. was a senior scientist for 21 years at Hughes, a U.S. defense contractor.

Dr. Kim was a design officer of NATO's missile defense system for potential threats from the Eastern Bloc during the Cold War era, a world-renowned authority in the field of artificial intelligence, and a scientist with extensive knowledge of the Pāli Suttas.[71] For ten years, he taught me in detail about the Early Buddhist discourses.

He was in Korea for about three years before returning to the United States, where I visited him several times. He kindly instructed me on the Pāli Suttas and meditation. With Dr. Kim, I visited various meditation centers in the U.S. including ones in California: the Ojai Meditation Center, the Samjin Meditation Center, and Self-Realization Fellowship Temple [YogĀnanda Meditation Center] in Pacific Pālisades. We visited Death Valley[72] and met up with meditators from Canada and Japan and

---

71 The Pāli Suttas [Early Buddhist discourses] are discourses written in Pāli. Pāli is the language most frequently used by the Buddha.

72 Death Valley National Park, also known as the valley of death, located in Eastern California near the Nevada border, has some of the most spectacular scenery in the world. This park has the lowest elevation of all the national parks in the U.S. [282 feet or 86 meters below sea level]. In the summer, a temperature of 120 F [49 C] or higher is typical.

exchanged information about the practice. I was impressed by these American meditation centers.

The words on the plaque at the Self-Realization Fellowship Temple are still vivid in my memory:

"Self-Realization Fellowship"

My appreciation for my great teacher, Dr. Kim, is as deep as the ocean.

— 33 —
Addiction

All phenomena in the universe are
Impermanent, suffering, and non-self,
Thus, an illusion,
Much like a desert mirage.
Anyone who does not know this illusion as an illusion,
That person will surely fall into ignorance and craving,
Much like being addicted to illicit drugs.[73]

I now know the truth of all things in the universe. All things arise dependent on causes and conditions and pass away dependent on causes and conditions.

We use labels or names like "I," "You," and "the World," in this stream of impermanence – this momentary arising and passing away. Therefore, I say, all things in the universe are empty, illusory, and impermanent.

Ven. Raṭṭhapāla realized Arahantship through the insight of the four kinds of wisdom:

1. "[Life in] any world is unstable, it is swept away
2. "[Life in] any world has no shelter and no protector
3. "[Life in] any world has nothing of its own
4. "[Life in] any world is incomplete, insatiate, the slave of craving"[74]

---

73 Mujin.
74 M82, the Raṭṭhapāla Sutta.

— 34 —
Nobles of Tibet

MILAREPA, A TIBETAN SAINT, WAS A DISCIPLE OF MARPA WHO always taught his disciples, "The world is an illusion, all things are illusions."

One day, Marpa's son died, and Marpa was crying and inconsolable. His disciples said to Marpa, "Teacher, you always taught us that all things are illusions. If this is the case, we do not understand why you are so sad about your son's death." Marpa replied, "My son's death is a greater illusion."

There are currently four major schools of Buddhism in Tibet: Nyingma, Kagyu, Sakya, and Gelug. Among these the one with the largest following is Gelug. The most well-known school to Europeans is Kagyu. Milarepa [1040–1123] belongs to the Kagyu school and the Dalai Lama, a Noble Laureate, belongs to the Gelug school.

— 35 —
Buddhism is the Science of Enlightenment

SOME MODERN PHYSICISTS HAVE ASSERTED THAT THE ONLY RELIgion compatible with science is Buddhism. What is science? It is simply knowing. This knowing is not based on faith; it is based on experimentation and verification. Buddhism of the Gautama Buddha is about "knowing and seeing" the Buddhist theory through experimentation and verification. Therefore, it is compatible with science.

Einstein, who is called the father of modern physics, said, "Buddhism has the characteristics of what would be expected in a cosmic religion for the future." Indeed, Buddhism explores far beyond other human religions on earth. Einstein also said, "Science without religion is lame, religion without science is blind."

> Salt prevents rotting because of its fundamental character, saltiness.
> The wind blows because of its fundamental character, movement.
> Truth is simple because of its fundamental character, simplicity.[75]

If one gives a complicated explanation about the truth of the Dhamma, one is contradicting oneself about the truth of the Dhamma: simplicity. James Watson, a biologist and a Nobel

---

75 Mujin.

laureate in Medicine 1962 for his co-discovery of the double helix structure of DNA, said, "truth is simple but elegant." The truth of the Dhamma is also simple but elegant. If a curious person listens to someone who really knows the Dhamma, he will quickly exclaim, "ah-ha!" This exclamation is a blessing of life and cannot be replaced with anything; only those who have experienced it know.

Einstein said, "Buddhism transcends a personal God, avoids dogmas and theology; it covers both the natural and spiritual; and it is based on a religious sense aspiring from the experience of all things, natural and spiritual, as a meaningful unity." Einstein also said, "I have deep faith that the principle of the universe will be beautiful and simple." This is the vision of the cosmos of a man who spent his life trying to understand the laws of natures.

I, Mujin, have made a lifelong effort to know the meaning of life through Buddhism, even if only for a moment. I believe that if I have a right understanding of the Four Noble Truths, the core of Buddhism, I will see the beautiful cosmic harmony within myself. Then if someone asks me; "What am I?" "Where do I come from?" and "Where am I going?" – perhaps, all of humanity's great questions – I will be able to answer without much difficulty.

Chade Meng Tan, previously a software engineer and current chairman of Search Inside Yourself Leadership Institute at Google, is well known for the mindfulness meditation course at Google and for his in-depth knowledge of Early Buddhism. He said, using the Dalai Lama's quote, "If science proves some belief of Buddhism wrong, then Buddhism will have to change."

— 36 —
Spacetime and Outside
of Spacetime

IN THE 1980S, A GROUP OF PHYSICISTS UNDER THE LEADERSHIP of the renowned French quantum physicist Alain Aspect, indirectly acknowledged the concept of the existence of a sphere "outside of spacetime" [which they referred to as "non-local phenomena"] in an experiment involving photons. This was the first time scientists in human history made such an acknowledgement.

Knowing this, how can spacetime [the relativistic and conditioned sphere] be explained? Although this theory created conflicts of opinion among modern theoretical physicists, they have not provided any basis to deny that a sphere outside of spacetime exists. This is what was indirectly suggested by Alain Aspect.

In the 1990s, a decade later, Amit Goswami, Ph.D., a retired professor from the physics department of the University of Oregon [1968–1997] in the United States, presented a compelling compromise. There is an anecdote that he received a big round of applause from theoretical physicists by suggesting that spacetime and "outside of spacetime" do not exist separately but rather co-exist. In time, Aspect's theory of "outside of spacetime" has received greater attention.

The above is from Dr. Edward Kim's lecture in Korea, "the Meditation of the Gautama Buddha and the Science of Enlightenment."

— 37 —
Law of Entropy

AMIT GOSWAMI, PH.D. SAID THAT NEITHER THE NON-LOCAL PHE-
nomena observed in the quantum world nor the wave equation
of Schrodinger [Austrian theoretical physicist, 1887–1961] could
be interpreted without the assumption of the existence of the
transcendental [outside of spacetime] sphere. In other words, the
primary consequence of spacetime is that all formed things will
disintegrate in space over time. This is called the law of entropy
in modern physics.

The Gautama Buddha called this phenomenon, "sabbe
saṅkhārā aniccā."[76] The Chinese say, "All conditioned things are
in a constant state of flux – impermanent."

In the "Song of Dharma Nature" [Beopseong gye], the Ven.
Bhikkhu Uisang of Silla[77] said the following:

> "The sphere of immutable truth and the sphere of conditioned
> phenomena co-exist, but it is only knowable by the enlight-
> ened one."[78]

---

76 Sabbe saṅkhārā aniccā [all conditioned phenomena are impermanent].
77 Silla is an ancient Korean kingdom [57 B.C.E.–935 C.E.].
78 Translated by Mujin.

— 38 —
Prayer Etched on Emile Bell [Divine Bell of King Seongdeok the Great]

"The divine bell [Shin Jong] has been created. Its shape is like a mountain, and its sound is like a dragon's hymn that reaches to the end of the earth and down to the underground . . . Wherever this bell is ringing, all evils shall be gone. Goodness shall rise, so that all humans and animals born in this nation may experience an awakening, like gentle ocean waves, and end their suffering."[79]

The glorious history of the ancient Silla kingdom is a history of Buddhist culture. Even after 1,300 years, the Divine Bell of King Seongdeok the Great still has an imposing and grand appearance. The prayer etched on the bell shows the Silla society's cherished desire for happier lives and their wish to end suffering. This prayer is relevant to our lives even now.

---

79 The prayer etched on the divine bell, Shin Jong of King Seongdeok the Great.

— 39 —
Dhamma

The Buddha realized and revealed the highest wisdom. The Buddha said, "This Dhamma that I have attained is profound, hard to see and hard to understand, peaceful and sublime, unattainable by mere reasoning, subtle, to be experienced by the wise."[80]

In Buddhism, when we speak of existence and non-existence, we do not mean that existence is something and non-existence is nothing. Depending on cause and condition, a phenomenon arises. Upon cessation of that cause and condition, the phenomenon passes away.

From existence to non-existence and from non-existence to existence, the interdependence or interrelations of all conditioned phenomena is called "paccaya." The arising and passing away of the five aggregates is called the [12 links] of dependent origination [paṭicca-samuppāda], also known as the origin and cessation of suffering.

---

80 M26:19, the Noble Search Sutta.

— 40 —
Common Sublime Principle of Humanity

THE HIGHEST ACHIEVEMENT OF LIFE IS THE REALIZATION OF Nibbāna, ultimate happiness. The Buddha lived and taught to show this to humanity. He was indeed a great teacher who embodied the truths.[81]

The Gautama Buddha – a great teacher of humans and devas – taught suffering, the origin of suffering, the cessation of suffering, and the way leading to the cessation of suffering. In other words, he showed us the path to Nibbāna, ultimate happiness. He tried mightily throughout his teaching career to show how to develop insight about oneself and to open one's eyes to the truths.

Those who understood the way leading to the cessation of ignorance [the cessation of suffering] that the Gautama Buddha had prescribed – those who followed the path and opened their eyes to the truths – found refuge in the Buddha, Dhamma, and Saṅgha.[82]

Two thousand six hundred years ago, or now, transcending spacetime, this Dhamma that shatters ignorance is within our reach. This Dhamma is the most valuable thing for all of humanity to know and share.

This phrase appears in the "Song of Dharma Nature" [Beopseong gye]:

---

81 The truths refer to the Four Noble Truths.
82 The Three Jewels of Buddhism.

"The sky is full of rain – a treasure for sentient beings!
The rain is collected by each person in his or her own
   vessel."[83]
[How much will your vessel hold?]

---

83 Translated by Mujin.

— 41 —
The Truth of the Being "I"

WHAT AM I? I AM A PILE OF THE FIVE AGGREGATES[84] [NAME-AND-form] that are mutually connected, dependent on conditions. The cause for the pile of the five aggregates is the volitional [kamma] formations.

> [SĀRIPUTTA] "Just as two sheaves of reeds might stand leaning against each other, so too, with name-and-form as condition, consciousness [comes to be]; with consciousness as condition, name-and-form [comes to be]."

> [BUDDHA] "Beings are owners of their actions, heirs of their actions; they originate from their actions, are bound to their actions, have their actions as their refuge."[85]

Although the five aggregates are but emptiness, it is tough to tear down the wall of the notion, "I," "mine," and "myself."

> "The five aggregates, mere floating clouds, aimlessly coming and going; Water bubbles of the three poisons, appear and disappear."[86]

---

84 The five aggregates are body and mind [feeling, perception, mental formations, consciousness]. They are also known as "materiality and mentality" or name-and-form.

85 M135.

86 The Song of Enlightenment [Zhèngdào gē], Ven. Bhikkhu Yeongga Hyeongak or Yongjia Zuanjue of the Tang Dynasty, China.

[BUDDHA] "Bhikkhus, whatever is not yours, abandon it. When you have abandoned it, that will lead to your welfare and happiness. And what is it, bhikkhus, that is not yours? Form[87] is not yours: abandon it. When you have abandoned it, that will lead to your welfare and happiness. Feeling is not yours ... Perception is not yours ... Volitional [mental] Formations are not yours ... Consciousness is not yours: abandon it. When you have abandoned it, that will lead to your welfare and happiness."[88]

---

87 Form refers to body.
88 S22:33, the Not Yours Sutta.

— 42 —
Age is Only a Numerical Concept

This bright light[89]
Tears down the conceptual wall!
Then, there is no trace of "I."
Who's been speaking of this "I," this "I'm?"
The light is not blue or red . . .
People quarrel about the details, saying,
"No! It's black! It's White!"
But the truth is, it is not a color at all.[90]

In his poem, "Youth," Samuel Ullman said, "Youth is not a time of life; it is a state of mind." Sometimes a person over 70 years old acts more youthful than a young man in his 20s. Age alone does not make a person young or old. Gen. MacArthur, who particularly liked Ullman's poem, had a copy of it along with a portrait of Abraham Lincoln hanging on his office wall. Gen. MacArthur is famous for saying, "Old soldiers never die, they just fade away."

Whether we are young or old, it is important to be in the present moment and not in the future or past.

---

89 One experiences the bright light through Buddhist meditation.
90 Mujin.

— 43 —
Laozi Says

"I have great tribulation
Because I have a body.
If I don't have a body,
What worries, and anxiety
Would there be for me?"[91]

Even as we are in the stream of impermanence, if we know the truth about impermanence, we feel neither sadness nor happiness.

"Have hearts of loving-kindness and compassion,
And keep your precepts;
Be energetic, resolute,
And always strong in exertion.

"Seeing heedlessness as fearful,
And heedfulness as security,
Develop the Noble Eightfold Path,
Realizing the deathless state."[92]

---

91 Laozi.
92 The Thag.17.1.979–980.

— 44 —
An Evening Glow at Simwu Sanbang

Today, at the edge of Dongnam mountain,
A deep red glow is draping the Shimwoo Sanbang.[93]
As the shadows of night draw near,
The birds in the yard are returning to their nests.
The chirping sound of a crake,
Throws a pebble into my quiet mind.[94]

---

93 The Shimwoo Sanbang is Mujin's home.
94 Mujin.

— 45 —
Hafiz, a Persian Saint and Poet

"Beside a river seat thee on the sward;
  It floweth past – so flows thy life away,
  So sweetly, swiftly, fleets our little day"[95]

Hafiz [1326–1389] also sang that one should stay awake and stay away from the self-consciousness. Even though people may be aware of Hafiz's meaning, they still stumble. The cause of their stumbling is volitional [kamma] formations.

The five aggregates are as insubstantial, hollow, and empty as the inner core of a plantain tree. When one eventually realizes that this world is nothing but illusions, the threat of death becomes powerless.

---

95 Poems from the Divan of Hafiz translated by Gertrude Lowthian Bell.

— 46 —
Realization of Impermanence [an Indomitable Mountaineer, Um, Hong Gil]

HONG GIL UM, AN INDOMITABLE MOUNTAINEER, IS KNOWN AS "the small tank of Himalayas." He was the first Asian to summit all 14 eight thousand meter peaks of the Himalayas and the Karakoram ranges in Asia, and he was the first person in the world to climb the 16 highest points on earth.

A reporter asked him, "It is difficult and dangerous to climb the 8,000-meter-peaks of the Himalayas even once in a lifetime. You climbed those peaks twenty times. What did you gain from such climbing and risking your life in doing so?" Um, Hong Gil replied, "I learned what impermanence is all about."

Now he tackles yet another, albeit metaphorical, mountain – [the Um Hong Gil] Human Foundation. This mountain does not belong to any continent, and it is higher and tougher than any peak on earth. Um, Hong Gil said, "I have been graced by the mountains that have allowed me to return from climbing unharmed. I want to return this blessing through [the Um Hong Gil] Human Foundation."

His plan is to work with several groups: boys and girls who are the heads of household, patients struggling with serious illnesses, and the spouses and children of Korean mountain climbers who could not afford any insurance and suffered debilitating injuries or death from mountain climbing. He wishes to provide hope for these groups by sharing his own climbing stories, climbing with patients, and opening schools in the Himalayan region.

He shares a mysterious, great medicine – a mountain – with people. He feels that in our materialistic society, we can only find peace and comfort in the great outdoors. I could tell from his compassionate statements that he has realized the truth of impermanence.

There are many who speak of impermanence and the non-self. However, some of these same people cannot take even one step forward because their legs are fettered by the concept of self – that which is without inherent existence or true essence. At times, these people say without hesitation, "Being too knowledgeable of the Dhamma can become an illness," to justify their ignorance. How could "knowing" be an illness? Ignorance is an illness. Didn't the Buddha say that because of ignorance, sentient beings suffer over and over from the cycle of birth, aging, illness, and death?

The ultimate purpose of Buddhist practice is to overcome ignorance. Therefore, the right view is revealed when we overcome ignorance through the correct understanding of the Buddha's teaching.

Indeed, fragrance emanates, and beauty shines from a person who has realized the noble truth of impermanence – like the mountaineer, Um Hong Gil as he takes one more step in extreme conditions.

— 47 —
Old Testament, the Book of Ecclesiastes

THERE IS A VERSE IN THE OLD TESTAMENT, THE BOOK OF ECCLE-siastes, "... Vanity of vanities! All is vanity."[96] I say, "All things are impermanent! Impermanent!"

Gosan, Seon Do Yun, a great poet of the Joseon Dynasty, rhapsodized in a stanza from his poem, Oh Wu Ga [Ode to Five Friends], about impermanence as follows:

> "Why do flowers fall soon after blossoming,
> Why do grasses turn brown soon after turning green,
> Perhaps the only unchanging thing is a rock."

Here is one of Shakespeare's sonnets:

> "Poor soul, the centre of my sinful earth,
> [Why feed'st] these rebel powers that thee array?
> Why dost thou pine within, and suffer dearth,
> Painting thy outward walls so costly gay?
> Why so large cost, having so short a lease,
> Dost thou upon thy fading mansion spend?
> Shall worms, inheritors of this excess,
> Eat up thy charge? Is this thy body's end?
> Then soul, live thou upon thy servant's loss,
> And let that pine to aggravate thy store;

---

96 Eccl 1:2 NIV.

Buy terms divine in selling hours of dross;
Within be fed, without be rich no more:
So shalt thou feed on Death, that feeds on men,
And, Death once dead, there's no more dying then."[97]

---

97 SparkNotes Editors. "SparkNote on Shakespeare's Sonnets." SparkNotes. com. SparkNotes LLC. 2002. Web. 28 Nov. 2019.

— 48 —
The Three Marks of Existence

THIS EARTH [SAHĀ-LOKA-DHĀTU] THAT I AM STANDING ON IS truly impermanent, unstable, and empty. So then, what meaning does this useless Sahā sphere have for me? Well, how marvelous it is that I can pass through the gate of liberation, utilizing the three characteristics of this useless Sahā sphere, impermanence, suffering, and non-self! That is why Seon [Zen] masters of antiquity called this Sahā sphere a great practice hall of enlightenment.

According to the Path of Purification, there are three gateways to liberation. These are known as impermanence, suffering, and non-self. "When one who has great resolution brings [formations] to mind as impermanent, one acquires the signless liberation. When one who has great tranquility brings [them] to mind as suffering, he acquires the desireless liberation. When one who has great wisdom brings [them] to mind as non-self, he acquires the void liberation."[98]

"Professor Jacques Maes is a world-renowned Swiss Buddhist scholar. He said that he first encountered Buddhism when he was ten years old in his parents' study. He was deeply moved upon seeing the words 'Prajñāpāramitā' in the book by Alexandra David-Néel [1868–1969].

"Alexandra David-Néel was a Belgian-French scholar and enthusiastic practitioner of Buddhism, who visited the Tibetan

---

98 Vis.XXI.70.

70

capital Lhasa for the first time when the colonial British authorities prohibited entry to Tibet.

"In 1968, before Alexandra David-Néel passed away at the age of 100, Prof. Jacques Maes visited her. Having returned from Japan, Prof. Jacques Maes was teaching at the University of Lausanne. Even at the age of 100, Alexandra David-Néel had a clear mind. She said that if you want to know Buddhism, you only need to know three things clearly: impermanence, suffering, and non-self. These three things are simple yet complicated. Because of one's ego, human beings suffer and always try to be someone or something. Therefore, we must strive to weaken our egos. In other words, we must always keep the concept of impermanence and suffering in our mind and abandon the concept of an enduring self so that we can realize the non-self.

"Alexandra David-Néel emphasized to Prof. Jacques Maes that it would be a grave mistake to think Buddhism is all about nihilism because of its focus on impermanence and suffering. It is illogical and unjust to apply absolute nihilism to Buddhism. Ven. Bhikkhu Youngsu [Nāgārjuna], a great philosopher of Buddhism, said that emptiness does not mean nothingness. In Buddhism, one does not say 'all exist, or all does not exist' or 'all is nothing.'

"The Gautama Buddha said, 'I understand the world, but the world does not understand me.'"[99]

I skip with joy when I meet a person who clearly understands the fundamentals of Buddhism.

---

99 [Walker, Who are You?] Authored by Hye Oak Jang and Sa Up Kim.

— 49 —
One Who is Worried about a Potential Loss

Friend, trembling with fear of potential loss!
If you have nothing now,
Such fear wouldn't exist.
Where are your possessions?
They are mere illusions projected by concepts,
Realize impermanence, suffering, non-self, and
Cross to the other shore of Nibbāna[100]

"Gate Gate Pāragate Pārasaṃgate Bodhi"[101]

[BUDDHA] "Bhikkhus, you may well acquire that possession that is permanent, everlasting, eternal, not subject to change, and that might endure as long as eternity. But do you see any such possession, bhikkhus: – No, venerable sir. – Good, bhikkhus. I too do not see any possession that is permanent, everlasting, eternal, not subject to change, and that might endure as long as eternity."[102]

---

100 Mujin
101 The Heart Sūtra.
102 M22:22, the Simile of the Snake Sutta.

—50—
The Verses of Arahant Rāhula and Arahant Ānanda

[Rāhula] "I am known as 'Fortunate Rāhula',
because I'm accomplished in both ways:
I am the son of the Buddha,
and I have the vision of the teachings.

"Since my defilements have ended,
since there are no more future lives
I'm perfected, worthy of offerings,
master of the three knowledges, seer of the deathless.

"Blinded by sensual pleasures, trapped in a net,
they are smothered over by craving;
bound by the Kinsman of the Negligent,
like a fish caught in a funnel-net trap.

"Having thrown off those sensual pleasures,
having cut Māra's bond,
and having plucked out craving, root and all:
I'm cooled, extinguished."[103]

[Ānanda] "When your friend has passed away,
and your Teacher is past and gone,
there's no friend like
mindfulness of the body.

---

103 Thag. 4.8.295–298, the Verses of Arahant Rāhula.

73

"The old has passed away,
  and I don't agree with the new.
Today I meditate alone
  like a bird snug in its nest."[104]

---

104 Thag.17.3.1041–1042, the Verses of Arahant Ānanda.

— 51 —
The Buddha Renounced the Life-Principle

IT IS RECORDED IN THE MAHĀPARINIBBĀNA SUTTA, "THREE months from now the Tathāgata [Buddha] will take final Nibbāna. So now, today, Ānanda, at the Cāpāla Shrine, the Tathāgata has mindfully and in full awareness renounced the life-principle."[105]

Then the Buddha said the following:

"Ripe I am in years. My lifespan's determined.
Now I go from you, having made myself my refuge.
Monks, be untiring, mindful, disciplined,
Guarding your minds with well-collected thought.
He who, tireless, keeps to law [teaching] and discipline,
Leaving birth behind will put an end to woe."[106]

When the Buddha told his disciples that he would take final Nibbāna in three months, Ven. Ānanda became most distraught and begged the Buddha to remain in the world longer. The Buddha said, "Ānanda, have I not told you before: All those things that are dear and pleasant to us must suffer change, separation and alteration? So how could this be possible? Whatever is born, become, compounded, is liable to decay – that it should not decay is impossible."[107]

---

105 D16:3.37.
106 D16:3.51.
107 D16:3.48.

The Buddha received his final meal from Cunda the Smith. To expel Cunda's remorse that his alms were the cause for the Buddha's final Nibbāna, the Buddha said the following verse:

[Buddha] "By giving, merit grows,
By restraint, hatred's checked.
He who's skilled abandons evil things.
As greed [lust], hate and folly wane, Nibbāna's gained."[108]

[Mujin] Your true friend is yourself.
But your enemy is also yourself.
One who rules one's mind well,
Becomes his own true friend.
But one who does not rule one's mind well,
Becomes his own enemy.
Do not let your true friend be
Controlled by lust·hatred·delusion.
If you do, your true friend becomes your enemy.[109]

---

108 D16:4.43.
109 Mujin.

— 52 —
Shakespeare's Sonnet 64

"Now that I have seen time's terrible hand
Deface the costly and splendid monuments
Of buried men from ages past,
And once-lofty towers torn down;
Now that I have seen even hard brass subject to
Perpetual destruction by human beings;
Now that I have seen the hungry ocean swallow up the land
And firm land seize territory from the ocean,
So that each one's loss is the other's gain;
Now that I have seen that
All things constantly change into something else
Or fall into decay
All this destruction has taught me to think:
The time will come in which time will take my love from me.
This thought feels like death and makes me weep over
What I have that I'm afraid of losing."[110]

Cui Bono

"What is Hope? A smiling rainbow
Children follow through the wet;
'Tis not here, still yonder, yonder:
Never urchin found it yet.

---

110 SparkNotes Editors. "SparkNote on Shakespeare's Sonnets." SparkNotes. com. SparkNotes LLC. 2002. Web. 28 Nov. 2019.

"What is life? A thawing iceboard;
On a sea with sunny shore; –
Gay we sail; it melts beneath us;
We are sunk, and seen no more.

"What is man? A foolish baby,
Vainly strives, and fights, and frets;
Demanding all, deserving nothing;
One small grave is what he gets."[111]

The English writer Thomas Carlyle said, "History is the essence of innumerable biographies." Did he also say that he would rather give up the Indian Empire than do without Shakespeare? One great person recognizes the greatness of another.

---

111 Thomas Carlyle [1795–1881], Critical and Miscellaneous Essays, Volume I: 1838.

— 53 —
Are All Things Created
by the Mind

CITTAMĀTRĀ, A SANSKRIT WORD, WAS TRANSLATED BY THE CHInese as yīqiè wéixīn zào. The source of this technical term traces back to Bhikkhu Asaṅga, a co-founder of the Yogācāra school. He was known to have used this term – consciousness-only – frequently, 1,000 years after the Buddha's passing. Consider this verse, "As a human being, if you want to know the spiritual sphere of the Buddha, you have to observe, you have to know that everything you see in the world comes from your own mind."[112] In other words, this simply means that "all phenomena are created by one's mind." This verse is widely known and often cited by Korean Buddhists.

Some people accept an exaggerated interpretation of this phrase and come up with great fiction! They liken the mind to the Christian God of all Creation based on the theory that "all phenomena are created by the mind."

In the Abhidhamma of Early Buddhism, it is stated that "the mind [citta] only knows." More specifically, consciousness arises when the sensory faculty comes in contact with the sense object. Simultaneously, consciousness and knowing arise like a sort of successive wave phenomenon. Therefore, it can be explained that "consciousness arises in dependence on the sense object;

---

112 The Flower Ornament Sūtra a.k.a. Hwaeom-gyeong, Huayan-jing, or Avataṃsaka Sūtra.

consciousness does not arise independently, without the sense object."

When a phenomenon is created in the mind, a phenomenon comes to be; when a phenomenon is removed from the mind, a phenomenon ceases;[113] It would be important to have the right understanding of the word "mind" in this verse when studying Buddhism. The word "mind" has many layers of meaning attached to it these days. Therefore, we must be careful not to apply a conventional meaning to the word when we are discussing an important theory of Buddhism.

> The moon in the sky,
> I look at the moon, then it looks at me.
> When I do not look at the moon,
> It does not look at me, either.
> So, the saying goes, "the world exists in my consciousness."[114]

---

113 Awakening of Faith in the Mahāyāna [Mahāyāna śraddhotpādaśāstra].
114 Mujin.

$-54-$
The Greatness of Descartes

DESCARTES [1596–1650], A FRENCH MATHEMATICIAN, AND BRIL-
liant philosopher said, "I think, therefore I am."[115] I like Descartes
very much. He noted that only mathematics was absolute among
the disciplines and that philosophy also must start from the absolute truth like mathematics. How could all religions on Earth be
exceptions to Descartes' assertion? He also said that the empty
mind is a space for unlimited creations.

---

115 The Discourse on the Method [French: Discours de la méthode], René
Descartes, 1637.

— 55 —
The World of the Philosopher Kant

THE GERMAN PHILOSOPHER KANT [1724–1804] WAS FASCINATED by Newtonian mechanics. He studied physics, mathematics, and philosophy at the university. He was also an astronomer and observed the sky using a telescope. Some who studied Kant's philosophy believed Kant thought that the mind plays an active role in structuring reality – in other words, that he believed the objective world didn't exist until perceived by the mind.

On his tombstone, the following phrases are engraved.

"Two things fill the mind with ever new and increasing admiration and awe, the more often and more steadily one reflects on them: the starry heavens above me and the moral law within me."

I respect Kant's philosophy very much. However, I sometimes disagree with his philosophy. About his view that body and mind are constrained within spacetime: I agree that the body is constrained within spacetime, but I do not agree that the mind is constrained within spacetime. The fact that the mind is not tied in spacetime was clarified by the Gautama Buddha two thousand six hundred years ago in the "threefold higher knowledge."[116]

---

116 The threefold higher knowledge: knowledge of the recollection of former life, knowledge of the divine eye, and knowledge of the destruction of the taints.

— 56 —
Heisenberg's Uncertainty Principle

HEISENBERG [1901–1976] WAS A GERMAN THEORETICAL PHYSICIST. In 1925, he published the theory of quantum mechanics. In 1932, he was awarded the Nobel Prize in Physics for the creation of quantum mechanics.

Heisenberg formulated new concepts about objectivity that hadn't been challenged since the time of Isaac Newton. Former scientific beliefs about objectivity did not work in quantum physics. According to the Heisenberg Uncertainty Principle, there is a fundamental limit to the precision with which certain pairs of physical properties of a particle [such as momentum and position], can be known. This theory raises a question as to the existence of an objective, independent reality that can be measured with precision.

Einstein said, "It seems as though we must use sometimes the one theory and sometimes the other, while at times we may use either. We are faced with a new kind of difficulty. We have two contradictory pictures of reality; separately neither of them fully explains the phenomena of light, but together they do."

The Buddha said about this perplexing question: "This world, Kaccāna, for the most part, depends upon a duality – upon the notion of existence and the notion of nonexistence. But for one who sees the origin of the world as it really is with correct wisdom, there is no notion of nonexistence in regard to the world. And for one who sees the cessation of the world as it really is with correct wisdom, there is no notion of existence in regard to the world."[117]

This duality is commonly expressed as the conventional reality [the notion of existence] and the ultimate reality [the notion of nonexistence] in Buddhism.

---

117 S12:15(5) the Kaccānagotta Sutta.

— 57 —
With a Hair's Breadth of Difference, the Distance would be like that Between Heaven and Earth

THE FAITHFUL MIND [XÌNXĪN MÍNG] WRITTEN BY VEN. BHIKKHU Seng-ts'an, the Third Chinese Chan [Seon] Patriarch, contains 146 verses, each of which is four characters, for a total of 584 characters. I really like this book. I am also particularly fond of the Song of Enlightenment [Zhèngdào gē] by Bhikkhu Yongjia. A verse in the Faithful Mind [Xìnxīn Míng] reads: "With a hair's breadth of difference, the distance would be like that between heaven and earth" [Háolí yǒu chā tiāndì xuángé].

A similar story can be found in the "Butterfly Effect of Chaos Theory" by Edward Lorenz, a mathematician and meteorology professor at the Massachusetts Institute of Technology. His theory states that a minute input change can produce a huge difference in the outcome. According to this theory, the flapping of a butterfly's wings in Brazil could potentially affect the atmospheric flow, leading to a tornado in Texas.

Using a computer, Dr. Lorenz performed the same calculations twice and got vastly different answers. Upon investigating the cause, he found that it was a minute input difference made by rounding off one variable by less than 0.0001. This discovery led to the publication of an academic paper, "Predictability: Does the Flap of a Butterfly's Wings in Brazil Set Off a Tornado in Texas?" in 1972.

— 58 —
Do Not Believe My Words

BUDDHISM IS A RELIGION OF SCIENCE AND ENLIGHTENMENT. IN other words, the path of enlightenment is not realized through blind faith but can be explored with scientific methods. The Buddha told us that we should not have to believe or agree with his words before we first test their validity. If we find his words to be true through our own practice [experimentation], we can then, and only then, should have confidence in his teaching. This teaching appears in the Ěrgēn Yuántōng of the Śūraṅgama Sūtra as the wisdom of listening, thinking, and practicing.

Therefore, many contemporary physicists and scientists who understand Buddhism call Buddhism, "the science of enlightenment" and the Gautama Buddha, "a scientist of enlightenment."

The ultimate objective of science is scientific knowledge, and one objective in the pursuit of scientific knowledge is to create better engineered machines, like planes, cars, ships, etc. Excellent engineering requires a thorough scientific understanding of the theory behind it. Technical terms must be understood. An ambiguous or vague sense of science will not produce good results! This, needless to say, is fundamentally understood by scientists.

Nowadays, I often see that in giving Dhamma sessions, many speakers talk about themselves instead of transmitting the teaching of the Buddha. They use abstract terms or explanations, making the Dhamma more challenging to understand. Buddhism is not abstract. More and more, modern science is proving the truths of Buddhism. Therefore, I would recommend that Buddhists turn their attention to science as well. Again, we need to ponder what the verses of the Faithful Mind [Xìnxīn Míng] and Dr. Lorenz's "Butterfly Effect" mean to us Buddhists.[118]

> The Ven. Bhikkhu Yongjia Xuanjue [Yeongga Hyeongak], the author of the Song of Enlightenment, said, "If I try to deceive sentient beings with a lie, let me endure the suffering of hell where my tongue is plucked out for eons as numerous as sand dust."

---

118 Gem No. 57: With a Hair's Breadth of Difference, the Distance would be like that Between Heaven and Earth.

— 59 —
A Mountain is a Mountain, Water is Water

IF WE SEE A MOUNTAIN AS A MOUNTAIN AND WATER AS WATER, we are only seeing them as concepts; we are not seeing them for what they really are. If we see things as concepts, we are not seeing them correctly. Because we do not see them correctly, suffering ensues.

All the core teaching of Early Buddhist discourses are contained in the Four Noble Truths and the Noble Eightfold Path. The Noble Eightfold Path means "the noble path with eight components." The correct and thorough understanding of the Four Noble Truths[119] is the first path [the right view] of the Noble Eightfold Path.

In science, if the theory is complicated, it will not be understood. Truth is always simple yet clear, just like Einstein's formula, $E = MC^2$.

What is the core teaching of Buddhism? The Four Noble Truths and the Noble Eightfold Path. There is nothing more to it. The Four Noble Truths and the Noble Eightfold Path are formulas of enlightenment, of deliverance from a cycle of life and death. Any other path to enlightenment would not be Buddhism of the Gautama Buddha. So, it is stated in the Mahāyāna Mahāparinirvāṇa Sūtra – On the Four Dependables – that we should not rely on people but rely on Dhamma; we should not rely on words but rely

---

119 Suffering, origin, cessation, and path.

on meaning; we should not rely on knowledge but rely on wisdom; we should not rely on incomplete teaching but rely on complete and clear teaching. Early Buddhist discourses define "complete and clear teaching" as the 37 Requisites of Enlightenment.

— 60 —
Seeing Clearly, There is Nothing to Be Seen

BUDDHISM TEACHES THAT THE ESCAPE FROM DEATH IS POSSIBLE. This is because the ultimate goal of Buddhism is Nibbāna. As explained in dependent origination, the realization of Nibbāna is possible by shattering ignorance. What scares human beings the most? Of course, it would be death. However, death does not really exist but is rather a delusion of discernment caused by ignorance. We know that death does not exist when we shatter ignorance. Therefore, Buddhism is a religion that shatters ignorance.

Consider this verse in the Song of Enlightenment [Zhèngdào gē 12:3]:

"Seeing clearly, there is nothing to be seen"

— 61 —
For the Fulfillment
of the Holy Life

"Thus, have I heard. On one occasion the Blessed One was dwelling among the Sakyans where there was a town of the Sakyans named Nāgaraka. Then the Venerable Ānanda approached the Blessed One. Having approached, he paid homage to the Blessed One, sat down to one side, and said to him:

[ĀNANDA] "Venerable sir, this is half of the holy life, that is, good friendship, good companionship, good comradeship.

[BUDDHA] "Not so, Ānanda! Not so, Ānanda! This is the entire holy life, Ānanda, that is, good friendship, good companionship, good comradeship. When a bhikkhu has a good friend, a good companion, a good comrade, it is to be expected that he will develop and cultivate the Noble Eightfold Path.

"And how, Ānanda, does a bhikkhu who has a good friend, a good companion, a good comrade, develop and cultivate the Noble Eightfold Path? Here, Ānanda, a bhikkhu develops right view, which is based upon seclusion, dispassion, and cessation, maturing in release. He develops right intention . . . right speech . . . right action . . . right livelihood . . . right effort . . . right mindfulness . . . right concentration, which is based upon seclusion, dispassion, and cessation, maturing in release. It is in this way, Ānanda, that a bhikkhu who has a good friend, a good companion, a good comrade, develops and cultivates the Noble Eightfold Path.

"By the following method too, Ānanda, it may be understood how the entire holy life is good friendship, good companionship, good comradeship: by relying upon me as a good friend, Ānanda, beings subject to birth are freed from birth; beings subject to aging are freed from aging; beings subject to death are freed from death; beings subject to sorrow, lamentation, pain, displeasure, and despair are freed from sorrow, lamentation, pain, displeasure, and despair. By this method, Ānanda, it may be understood how the entire holy life is good friendship, good companionship, good comradeship."[120]

The Buddha said that a true Brahmin is one who practices the Noble Eightfold Path [morality·concentration·wisdom] and not the one who recites Veda and mantras.[121]

---

120 S45:2, the Half the Holy Life Sutta.
121 D1:3, the Ambaṭṭha Sutta: About Ambaṭṭha.

— 62 —
What is the Holy Life

[BHADDA] "Friend Ānanda, it is said, 'the holy life, the holy life.' What now, friend, is the holy life, and who is a follower of the holy life, and what is the final goal of the holy life?

[ĀNANDA] "This Noble Eightfold Path, friend, is the holy life; that is, right view . . . right concentration. One who possesses this Noble Eightfold Path is called a liver of the holy life. The destruction of lust, the destruction of hatred, the destruction of delusion: this, friend, is the final goal of the holy life."[122]

From the Vajrasamādhi:[123] "Upāsaka [lay follower], there is a lake called Anavatapta[124] in the middle of Perfume mountain. The water there has eight different flavors, and anyone who drinks the water will be cured of illness. Likewise, the Vajrasamādhi has eight kinds of the right path,[125] and Bodhisattva[126] will cut off all taints upon earnestly practicing them."[127]

---

122 S45:20, the Cock's Park Sutta.

123 The author of the Vajrasamādhi is unknown. The first commentary of this sūtra, "Exposition of Vajrasamādhi Sūtra" was written by Ven. Bhikkhu Wonhyo [617–686] of Silla, the ancient kingdom of Korea.

124 According to an ancient legend, Anavatapta is a lake in the middle of the Perfume Mountain in the Himalayas.

125 The Noble Eightfold Path.

126 Bodhisattva is one who is walking the path to enlightenment while educating sentient beings. See gem no. 67 for detailed information about the meaning of Bodhisattva.

127 The "Meaning of Vajrasamādhi," authored by Jae Guen Kim, October 1980.

— 63 —
The Meaning of the Path of Purification

THE PATH OF PURIFICATION, AUTHORED BY VEN. BUDDHAGHOSA in the 5th century C.E., is an indisputable comprehensive treatise on Southern [Theravāda] Buddhist doctrine.

In this book, Ven. Buddhaghosa explained the teaching of the suttas by first presenting "the five paths of purification."[128] This is followed by a brief commentary that the Path of Purification consists of morality·concentration·wisdom. He explains in the Path of Purification there are three gateways to liberation:[129] the signless liberation, the desireless liberation, and the void liberation through the insight of impermanence, suffering, and non-self.

He also said to guard against the inversion of perception, "Better, bhikkhus, the extirpation of the eye faculty by a red-hot burning blazing glowing iron spike than the apprehension of signs [nimitta] in the particulars of visible objects cognizable by the eye."[130] In the Saṁyutta Nikāya, which is a collection of the Buddha's teaching organized by subject matter, perception is compared to an "incorporeal shimmering mirage." In other words, perception is truly "void, hollow, and insubstantial."[131] The Buddha's true disciple who walks the path to Nibbāna must

---

128 Vis.I.6, 1) Insight alone, 2) Jhana and understanding, 3) Deeds [kamma], 4) Morality, 5) the Foundations of mindfulness.
129 Vis.XXI.70.
130 Vis.I.100.
131 S22:95.

ONE MAN'S JOURNEY TOWARD ENLIGHTENMENT

know which perception to keep and which perception to abandon. Only then will he realize revulsion, dispassion, and deliverance, through the deep understanding that perception has the characteristics of impermanence, suffering, and non-self.

Hegel [1770–1831], known as an idealist philosopher of Germany, said that perception already contains internal contradictions.

— 64 —
Who is a Learned and Wise Disciple

[BUDDHA] "One who is deluded, overcome by delusion, with the mind obsessed by it, intends for his own affliction, for the affliction of others, or for the affliction of both, and he experiences mental suffering and dejection. But when delusion is abandoned, he does not intend for his own affliction, for the affliction of others, or for the affliction of both, and he does not experience mental suffering and dejection. It is in this way, too, that Nibbāna is directly visible."[132]

A foolish one sells today's living to buy tomorrow's death;
A learned, wise disciple burns today's living;
With that fire, one burns the death of tomorrow.[133]

---

132 A3:55, the Nibbāna Sutta.
133 Mujin.

— 65 —
Modern Science's Five
Methods of Proof

What is the meaning of religion? There are many religions in this world. In my opinion, most of these religions aim to provide sublime teaching to humanity. To accomplish this, however, I think religion must acknowledge the value of human life and lead followers to reach their full spiritual potential.

In Buddhism, this process is the transformation of human consciousness from a state of ignorance to clear knowledge, through the understanding of the Four Noble Truths. Under the Buddha's methodology, the process of transformation must be explained clearly. The expected outcome should be attainable by following the teaching prescribed by the Buddha. I believe, the Buddha's methodology is like 21st century science.

So, what is the purpose of human life? I believe one common goal of all humans is happiness. The Buddha said ordinary happiness and ultimate happiness [enlightenment] are possible when humans base their lives on the clear knowledge of the Four Noble Truths. Such sublimated consciousness allows humans to see themselves and the world correctly. As clear knowledge develops and matures, ordinary and ultimate happiness grow proportionally.

Wholesome consciousness results in wholesome culture and unwholesome consciousness results in unwholesome culture. Wholesome consciousness leads to wholesome deeds: compassion, loving-kindness, thoughtfulness, dedication, and charity.

Unwholesome consciousness produces self-centeredness, or in other words, lust, hatred, and delusion [the three poisons].

Through his own enlightenment process, the Buddha attained the "threefold higher knowledge"[134] 2,600 years ago. As a result, he clearly understood the value of human life, ordinary happiness and ultimate happiness [enlightenment]. He defined the theory and practice by which humans could discover their full spiritual potential. This is explained in the Four Noble Truths.

There are many ways in science to prove a theorem. A scientific method of proof is not easy to define! The following methods are but five among many used by modern science.

The first method is called the Definitional Proof. A name, or designation, is given to an object: a man, a woman, a chairman, a president, a single lady, a married lady, etc. For instance, when a lady is married, she is called a married lady. This cannot be denied because the label itself defines the lady. This is a Definitional Proof.

A second method is called the Logical Proof. In mathematics, 1×0 equals 0; this cannot be denied because of its logic. This method is called the Logical Proof.

A third method is called the Experimental Proof. For example, water reaches the boiling point at $100\ ^{\circ}C$ under the atmospheric pressure at sea level [1 bar]. Anyone who performs the same experiment will obtain the same result. This method is called the Experimental Proof.

A fourth method is the Observational Proof. This is used in astronomy. For example, it takes 365 days for the Earth to orbit the Sun. This determination was made through continuous observation of the rotation and revolutions of Earth, and by viewing solar and lunar eclipses. This method is called the Observational Proof.

---

134 The "threefold higher knowledge" refers to knowledge of the recollection of former life, knowledge of the divine eye, and knowledge of the destruction of the taints.

A fifth method is called the Evidential, or Judicial Proof. This is often used in apprehending criminals. Investigation of fingerprints, alibis, statements of witnesses, DNA analysis, etc., are all used in the Judicial Proof.

I think that explanations of Buddhist theory most resemble the Definitional and Logical Proof. I think explanations about Buddhist practice follow most closely the Experimental and Observational Proof. If Buddhism can be called "scientific," this means that anyone who learns Buddhist theory and practice it accordingly should achieve the same result – ordinary happiness and ultimate happiness [enlightenment]. The Buddha said as much in the suttas.

If I were a Buddhist scientist, I would add a sixth method of proof to the above list. It would be called the Buddhist Meditational Proof.

— 66 —
The Right Knowledge of Buddhism is an Essential Guide to the Right Practice

NEEDLESS TO SAY — AND IT HAS BEEN SAID REPEATEDLY — CORE teaching of Buddhism is the Noble Eightfold Path.

Each component or path of the Noble Eightfold Path begins with the word "right," However, it is seldom that I meet someone who understands the simple meaning of "right" correctly. I came to this conclusion based on my discussions about the true meaning of the Noble Eightfold Path with those Koreans who have studied Buddhism for many years. There are probably two reasons for this:

First, the root of all Buddhist Discourses [suttas or sūtras] is the Early Buddhist Discourses. These are the five Pāli Nikāyas of Southern Theravāda Buddhism and the four Sanskrit Āgama Discourses of Northern Buddhism. However, the Early Buddhist Discourses were largely unavailable, and thus unknown, to most Koreans. Instead, Koreans embraced Chinese Buddhism[135] which has been heavily influenced by Chinese culture and Mahāyāna Buddhism. Mahāyāna Buddhism was established in South India in the first century C. E. When these two kinds of Buddhism spread to Korea, their sūtras and literature were accepted by Koreans as the authentic teaching of the Buddha.

---

135 See gem number 70, Chinese Buddhism.

Second, the Buddha sometimes used "ultimate" language [paramattha-desanā] for his teaching, to guide ignorant sentient beings to realization. This "ultimate" language is a transcendent language [Chinese translation: 最勝義]. It would be a grave mistake to interpret the Buddha's teaching using the commonly accepted meanings of words that we use now in everyday life. Even though the words are spelled the same, their conventional meaning is quite different from their true, "ultimate" meaning. Interchanging the conventional with the "ultimate" meaning of these words could result in vast discrepancies of meaning! The language of transcendence is the language of the Buddha. After his enlightenment, during his 45-years of teaching, he used this transcendent language to create the technical terms for the edification of sentient beings. The Buddha's explanation of the Noble Eightfold Path uses this "ultimate" language.

There must be a way to communicate in such "ultimate" language with those who have not experienced [knowing, seeing, and experiencing] even once the sphere of transcendence of phenomena. However, using the conventional language of the Sahā world, the conceptual sphere, communication [correct understanding] would be limited. So, the Buddha used an existing dialect commonly used among people at that time. He replaced, supplemented, or refined the meaning of existing words. He created a language by infusing knowledge from the sphere of transcendence into the existing local dialect. This allowed him to communicate with sentient beings. This language is called Pāli: the transcendent, noble language of the Buddha. Later, Buddhist scholars quipped that the Buddha "puts new liquor in the old sack."

The ultimate goal of science is scientific knowledge, and through such knowledge, many conceptual objects, like automobiles, airplanes, ships, and computers, are produced. Likewise, Buddhism's "right" practice must have the foundation of "right" knowledge.

The Buddha taught us key technical terms to shatter our ignorance and to lead us to the shore of deliverance·Nibbāna. Only when we understand the exact meaning of each phrase [of the Buddha's teaching], can we practice correctly and so arrive at the hoped-for destination, deliverance·Nibbāna.

For details on the Noble Eightfold Path, see Appendix II – Path to Deliverance·Nibbāna: The Four Noble Truths and The Noble Eightfold Path.

Practice without the benefit of the right theory is dangerous. Understanding theory without having the benefit of practice is like drinking water from an empty glass. If you understand the right theory, it is like having clear eyesight. If you practice, it is as if you're being given feet. If we only walk with feet but are sightless, we might drown in a river, or fall off a cliff. However, if we only have eyes and do not have feet with which to walk, we would never reach our destination.

Understanding the right theory is like knowing the traffic rules that tell pedestrians to stop at the red light and cross at the green light. The right practice is like having eyes that can differentiate color. In other words, even if we can differentiate a green light from a red light, we will be in danger of crossing the street without knowledge of the traffic rules. Conversely, with the knowledge of the traffic rules, but without the ability to discern a red from a green light, results would be disastrous!

So, in Buddhism, "knowing and seeing the reality as it is" is essential. If Buddhism is compared to science, the "theory" could be equated with scientific knowledge, and the "practice" could be equated to experimentation.

− 67 −
Who is the Avalokiteśvara Bodhisattva

THE AVALOKITEŚVARA BODHISATTVA IS A PROMINENT BODHISATtva, well known among Buddhists in Korea, China, and Japan.

The Avalokiteśvara Bodhisattva appears in the following sūtras of Mahāyāna Buddhism:

- The Lotus Sūtra, Chapter 25: The Universal Gateway of the Avalokiteśvara Bodhisattva.
- The Flower Ornament Sūtra, Chapter on Entry into the Sphere of Reality [Sudhanakumâra meets the Avalokiteśvara Bodhisattva, the 27th reliable spiritual teacher among 53 such teachers.]
- The Śūraṅgama Sūtra [The Buddha told the Avalokiteśvara Bodhisattva to realize Samādhi through hearing.]
- The short version of the Heart Sūtra which is the summary of the 600 volumes of Mahāprajñāpāramitā Sūtra.

The Avalokiteśvara Bodhisattva appears only once in the short version of the Heart Sūtra. This fact was first discovered by a Buddhist scholar, Dr. Daisetsu T. Suzuki [1870–1966]. Dr. Suzuki studied at Tokyo Senmon Gakko [the predecessor of Waseda University]. In 1897, he went to America on his teacher Soyen Shaku's recommendation. After staying in America for a decade, he returned to Japan in 1909. He lectured at Tokyo Imperial University, then in 1921, he became a professor at Otani University and devoted himself to the research of Buddhism. He published numerous books and was instrumental in spreading Zen Buddhism to the West.

According to Buddhist scholars, the Avalokiteśvara Bodhisattva first appears in the 1st century C.E. Mahāyāna Sūtras as a deva. The Avalokiteśvara Bodhisattva is not found in any Buddhist discourses prior to the 1st century C.E.[136] Needless to say, the short version of the Heart Sūtra – in which both the Avalokiteśvara Bodhisattva and the Gautama Buddha appear – is not historically accurate. However, the Avalokiteśvara Bodhisattva clearly explains how to achieve liberation, or, in other words, the realization of wisdom through the Gautama Buddha's teaching of the Four Noble Truths and the Nobel Eightfold Path [morality·concentration·wisdom].

The Philosopher's Path in Kyoto was named by Kokusyo Iwao [1895–1949], a professor at Kyoto University, in 1920. It was said that he modeled the Philosopher's Path in Kyoto after the Philosopher's Walk in Heidelberg, Germany. In 1970, the city of Kyoto turned the path into a park. Since then, the Philosopher's Path is well known and has attracted many tourists. The path runs 1.8 km from the Nyakuoji Bridge to the Ginkakuji-Bashi Bridge. Nishida Kitaro [1870–1945] – a prominent Japanese philosopher, a professor at Kyoto University, and a friend of Dr. Suzuki – walked this path often as he worked on establishing the Kyoto School of Philosophy between 1930–1940. He drew his original thinking from both Zen Buddhism and Western philosophies. This movement remains influential in Japanese society today.

---

136 See gem number 68, Mahāyāna Buddhism.

— 68 —
Mahāyāna Buddhism

ALTHOUGH MAHĀYĀNA BUDDHISM IS MENTIONED IN LITERATURE from the 1st–2nd centuries B.C.E., it reached the height of its popularity around the 1st century C.E. in South India. Let's briefly take a look at its history. About 100 years after the Gautama Buddha's passing [parinibbāna] at 483 B.C.E. [alternate possible date: 544 B.C.E.], the Buddhist Saṅgha splits into Sthaviravāda/ Theravāda [conservative Buddhism] and Mahāsāṃghikas [progressive Buddhism]. This split is called the first schism and was followed by many subsequent divisions in both schools. The result of these divisions was that there were approximately 20 schools of Buddhist thoughts by the 1st century B.C.E.

Buddhism from the period – 100 years after the Gautama Buddha's passing through the 1st century B.C.E. – is called Nikāya Buddhism. Buddhism before this period, is called Primitive Buddhism, Fundamental Buddhism, or Early Buddhism.

The extreme schismatic process of Nikāya Buddhism drew criticism from lay Buddhists who thought that monastics cared only about their own Nibbāna and ignored the liberation of the laity. These monastics were referred to as belonging to the "Lesser Vehicle" or Hīnayāna Buddhist sect. In response to this criticism, a new Buddhist movement, in which monastics put laity's salvation ahead of their own enlightenment, was created. This movement emphasized improving the condition of both the monastics and laity through the performance of good deeds. These monastics were called "Bodhisattvas" and were considered ideal human beings. They claimed that they were transmitting the true teaching of the Buddha. They called their movement the "Great Vehicle" or Mahāyāna Buddhism.

The Mahāyāna Sūtras, which supposedly contained the true meaning of the Buddha's teaching, began to be compiled four to five hundred years after the Buddha's passing. These include the Lotus Sūtra [the Saddharma Puṇḍarīka Sūtra], the Perfection of Wisdom Sūtra [the Prajñāpāramitā Sūtra], the Nirvana Sūtra, the Ten Stages Sūtra [the Daśabhūmika Sūtra], the Mahāvaitulya Sūtra, and the Immeasurable Life Sūtra [the Vimalakīrti Nirdeśa Sūtra]. The Diamond Sūtra was published in the 3rd century C.E.; the Flower Ornament Sūtra was published in the 4th century C.E. in Khotan, an ancient Buddhist kingdom of Central Asia. The Mahāprajñāpāramitā Sūtra began around the 1st century C.E. and was completed over a period of 1,200 years.

However, Mahāyāna Buddhism declined from the 5th to 6th century C.E. and slowly morphed into a tantric religion, which continued until the 12th century C.E. Thereafter, it was assimilated into the Hindu religions of both the masses and minor sects. Currently in India the Gautama Buddha is worshipped as the 9th incarnation of Vishnu, one of the three main Hindu gods who maintains the universe.

The Mahāyāna Sūtras were written over a period of 1,000 years, beginning four to five hundred years after the Gautama Buddha's passing. The Tantric Sūtras were compiled between the 7th–10th century C.E. However, no records exist of when, where, or who compiled the Mahāyāna Sūtras.

These early Mahāyāna writers were extremists and few in number. As previously noted, they referred to their movement as the "Great Vehicle" [Mahāyāna], and they disparagingly referred to anyone who challenged their views as being from the "Lesser Vehicle," [Hīnayāna]. Nevertheless, monastics belonging to Mahāyāna and Hīnayāna commonly lived in the same temple. Mahāyāna Buddhists – in competition with the Hindu Bhakti movement – built magnificent temples and filled them with enormous Buddha and Bodhisattva statues. Deities such as the Amitabha, Avalokiteśvara Bodhisattva, Bhaiṣajyaguru [Medicine Tathāgata], Mahāvairocana Tathāgata, and countless others came from this period. As F. Th. Stcherbatsky, a Russian Indologist and Buddhist scholar from St. Petersburg University persuasively pointed out, Mahāyāna Buddhists created a whole new religion and made the Gautama Buddha into a supernatural, transcendent god.

Avalokiteśvara is a Sanskrit word, and Sanskrit is an ancient Indian language. The Ven. Kumārajīva of the Kingdom of Kucha translated "Avalokiteśvara" as Guānshìyīn [觀世音]. The Ven. Xuanzang translated it as Guānzìzài [觀自在]. Regardless of the variation of translations, the meaning of this title is the "Lord who gazes down on the world with bright light and compassion."

When this new religion, Mahāyāna Buddhism, was being launched in earnest in the 1st century C.E., many devas were incorporated into Mahāyāna Buddhism. One of these devas was Avalokiteśvara Bodhisattva. Since then the Avalokiteśvara Bodhisattva went through personification, deification, and became a subject of deep faith to many people. The world's leading Buddhist scholars have not denied this historical fact.

I, myself, was drawn to Avalokiteśvara, who represents compassion. I also like the Sudhanakumâra, a young attendant of Avalokiteśvara Bodhisattva.

"Avalokiteśvara Bodhisattva clad in white
speaks without speaking,
Sudhanakumāra hears without hearing.
Willow in the bottle of sacred nectar is
summer in three-periods,[137]
green bamboo in front of the rock is spring in all worlds."[138]

---

137 Three periods: past, present, and future.
138 Seo Do Jib, authored by Bhikkhu Kyung Bong.

The word "Bodhisattva" is a compound Sanskrit word. "Bodhi" means awakening or enlightenment and "sattva" means existence, or sentient being. During the Nikāya Buddhism period "Bodhisattva" meant a seeker of enlightenment or a religious practitioner who is likely to become a Buddha in future lives. In Mahāyāna Buddhism, "Bodhisattva" has two meanings: "seeking enlightenment from above," and "edifying sentient beings below." Alternatively, or to put it more simply, the "Bodhisattva" is one who "practices to improve his or her own condition as well as that of the laity."

— 69 —
Tantric Buddhism

MAHĀYĀNA BUDDHISM REACHED THE HEIGHT OF POPULARITY IN the 1st century C.E. However, about five to six hundred years later, its following began to decline, and it eventually evolved into Tantric Buddhism [Esoteric Buddhism]. This is when the Tantric Sūtras, filled with many mantras, began to appear. The Tantric practitioners used sexual practices between a man and a woman as a way to achieve Buddhahood. Tantric Buddhism was established in the middle of the 7th century C.E. and lasted until the 12th century C.E. As previously stated, there was a point in time when there was no difference between Tantric Buddhism and some sects of Hinduism, which was the popular religion of the masses. In the end, Tantric Buddhism was wholly absorbed into Hinduism. So, the practice of Mahāyāna Buddhism declined from the 4th century C.E. due to the influence of Hinduism. Today, because of other influences, such as that of Islam, the practice of Mahāyāna Buddhism has become completely wiped out in India.
What is Tantra?

1. Originally, Tantra started in and around Tibet, where the desire to obtain enlightenment through visualization had been practiced. Later, as India's Mahāyāna Buddhism declined, Tantra spread widely to the region west of China. Indian Tantric Buddhism merged with Hinduism. It started to show signs of corruption, most notably when the meditation practice was combined with the worship of sexual energy [shakti].

2. Tantric literature refers to the writing of a sect that worships sexual energy. This sect belongs to Shaivism, which exists within the Hindu religion. It is widely believed that most Tantric literature was written between the 7th and 10th centuries C.E.

— 70 —
Chinese Buddhism

THE BUDDHIST DISCOURSES FROM INDIA GRADUALLY MADE THEIR way to China between the 2nd and 3rd centuries C.E. Translation of these discourses began in earnest between the 3rd and 6th centuries C.E.

For some reason, Indians did not reveal the dates and authors of their discourses. The Mahāyāna and Tantric [Esoteric] discourses begin with the phrase, "Thus have I heard" – much the same way as did the Pāli and Āgama discourses. The Ven. Ānanda, a cousin of the Gautama Buddha, who lived for most of his adult life with the Buddha, is thought to be the "I" in "Thus have I heard." Therefore, the Chinese may have assumed the discourses from India that begin, "Thus have I heard" to be the words of the Gautama Buddha.

The discourses of Mahāyāna and Esoteric Buddhism were not transmitted to China in any historical order. Instead, they came randomly. Vast numbers of texts, assumed to be the written words of the Gautama Buddha, were written by various people over nearly one thousand years and disseminated in China.

China and India have different cultures and entirely different languages. Also, the human experiences contained in the vast number of Indian Buddhist discourses are altogether different from those of the Chinese. Therefore, I believe that those who attempt to translate the discourses from the Indian language to the Chinese language need to meet at least three qualifications. First, the translator must be proficient with both the Indian and

Chinese languages! Second, the translator must truly understand the content of the discourses – both literally and experientially. Third, the translator must be devoted to his or her own meditation practice. If these qualifications are not met, mistranslation is inevitable.

So, how many ancient Chinese translators met all these qualifications? Initially, the Chinese Daoists translated the Buddhist discourses as they understood it, through their Daoist experience. This is called géyì, a translation which ultimately reframes the original meaning. Later, the Ven. Kumārajīva, an Indian monk from Central Asia, and the Ven. Xuanzang, a Chinese Buddhist scholar-monk produced more accurate translations.

Nonetheless, the result was that the Chinese Buddhist discourses, referred to as the Chinese Buddhist canon, directly reflected Chinese influence. For instance, in the Chinese Buddhist canon, the names of people were changed: Vasubandhu became Shìqīn, Vasubandhu's brother Asanga became Wúzhuó. Ven. Kumārajīva translated Avalokiteśvara as Guānshìyīn Púsà; Ven. Xuanzang translated Avalokiteśvara as Guānzìzài Púsà.

Upon reading the Chinese Buddhist canon, I feel that many texts do not make sense in content or style. Consider the following contradictions:

The Ven. Tiantai Zhiyi endeavored to organize the Chinese Buddhist canon by both content and historical chronology. This is referred to as Zhiyi's taxonomy or classification system. He reached the following conclusion from his research: the Gautama Buddha divided his teaching career of 45 years [or 50 years according to the Ven. Tiantai Zhiyi] into five periods. During his final eight years, the Gautama Buddha taught the Lotus Sūtra, which then was kept in the underwater palace of the Dragon King. Later on, Ven. Nāgārjuna [Yongsu] supposedly brought it out from the sea palace. Ven. Tiantai Zhiyi concluded that the Lotus Sūtra is the best among all sūtras.

Based on his interpretation of the Lotus Sūtra, he founded an entire sect of Buddhism – the Tiantai sect.

Or, consider the following example: Supposedly, three weeks after the Gautama Buddha's enlightenment, the Buddha taught his first discourse – the Flower Ornament Sūtra – to six thousand "Virtually Enlightened Bodhisattvas" who suddenly appeared. This sūtra was also kept in the underwater place of the Dragon King until the Ven. Nāgārjuna brought it out, thereby making it the most important among all sūtras in the Chinese Buddhist canon. Based on this premise, the Flower Ornament school [Hwaeom Jong] was established.

Although, these two sūtras start with the phrase, "Thus Have I Heard," the Lotus Sūtra, which was written by Mahāyāna Buddhists, dates from the 1st century C.E., which is five hundred years after the Gautama Buddha's passing. The Flower Ornament Sūtra was published in the ancient Khotan kingdom of Central Asia in the 4th century C.E. or nine hundred years after the Gautama Buddha's passing. It is most likely that the Chinese may not have known that these sūtras were composed hundreds of years after the Buddha's passing since both sūtras begin with the phrase, "Thus Have I Heard." The Chinese would have believed this "I" to be the Ven. Ānanda, who was contemporaneous with the Gautama Buddha.

These are just two examples of how Chinese Buddhist sects, all based on Mahāyāna Buddhism, were founded.

The main sects of Chinese Buddhism include Chan [Seon], Tiantai, Hwaeom, Pure Land, Three-Treatise, Dharma-Character, Vinaya, and True Word. Chan [Seon] Buddhism, alone, has split into five schools and seven sects.

Unquestionably, Chinese Buddhism is a creation of Chinese genius, a legacy of Chinese culture. Chinese Chan [Seon] Buddhism's origin is a combination of Daoist culture and Buddhism; Pure Land Buddhism's origin is a combination of Northern Chinese Shamanism and Buddhism.

— 71 —
Hīnayāna Buddhism

I OFTEN HEAR THE DISPARAGING TERM, HĪNAYĀNA BUDDHISM, from those who are familiar with Mahāyāna Buddhism. They believe in very literal meanings of the words Mahāyāna [Great Vehicle] and Hīnayāna [Lesser Vehicle]. The Mahāyāna Buddhists' ultimate purpose and ideal are twofold: putting the salvation of sentient beings ahead of their own enlightenment by remaining on Earth as Bodhisattvas and helping sentient beings by practicing the six Pāramitās.[139]

It was not uncommon for Mahāyāna Buddhists to criticize Hīnayāna Buddhists for their goal of achieving the Buddhahood only for themselves. However, if one looks closely, there is no actual evidence that there was an official practice of what was referred to as Hīnayāna Buddhism in the two thousand six hundred year history of Buddhism. The term Hīnayāna can be traced back to four to five hundred years after the Buddha's passing. During this time, Mahāyāna monastics – while creating the Mahāyāna Sūtras – referred disparagingly to their fellow monastics who disagreed with them as being Hīnayāna. Yet, they all lived in the same temple.

Was there ever a monastic or lay Buddhist who called himself or herself a Hīnayāna Buddhist? I have never seen any evidence of this among the many historical discourses and literature written about Buddhism.

---

139 Six Pāramitās refer to generosity, morality, endurance, effort, concentration, wisdom [Dāna, Śīla, Kṣānti, Vīrya, Dhyāna, Prajñā].

So, although Hīnayāna Buddhism has never actually existed as an official practice, Theravāda Buddhism – a sect of Buddhism that succeeded the direct disciples of the Buddha – has existed from one hundred years after the Buddha's passing to the present time. It certainly existed before the beginning of Mahāyāna Buddhism. Theravāda Buddhism – also known as Southern Buddhism or Early Buddhism – has been transmitted by Theravāda monastics and continues to be transmitted, intact, in many parts of the world.

The five Nikāyas of Pāli discourses contain the Buddha's authentic voice. Japan's Taishō Shinshū Daizōkyō – the world's most extensive collection of Buddhist discourses – was completed through collective efforts of the Japanese academia over thirteen years [1912–1925]. This collection was modeled after the TriPiṭaka Koreanna.[140] The Japanese collection is about twice as big as the TriPiṭaka Koreana. The Japanese collection includes the compilation of the TriPiṭaka Koreana, discourses written in Sanskrit, and discourses of Chinese translation. It is compiled and organized into the following sections: Mahāyāna and Theravāda – Sutta, Vinaya, and Abhidhamma. In addition, this collection includes annotations that explain the difference between the Indian and Chinese discourses. A decade later, from 1935 to 1941, the original Pāli texts were translated into 60 or 70 volumes called the Nanden Daizōkyō. These volumes correspond to these five Nikāyas:

The Dīgha Nikāya: the Collection of Long Discourses
The Majihima Nikāya: the Collection of Middle-length
    Discourses
The Saṁyutta Nikāya: the Collection by Thematically linked
    Discourses
The Aṅguttara Nikāya: the Numerical Discourses
The Khuddaka Nikāya: the Minor Collection

---

140 The TriPiṭaka Koreanna, also known as Palman-daejang-gyeong is a Korean collection of Buddhist texts carved onto 80,000 wooden printing blocks in the 13th century.

Science and civilization have advanced in the 21st century, at times exceeding our wildest imagination. As science and civilization evolve, the Buddha's teaching [Dhamma] is being recognized as a treasure trove of solutions to fundamental issues, including the future direction of humanity and the relationship between the universe and human beings. Buddhism remains a beacon of hope, a torch, and a lighthouse for all humankind.

— 72 —
About Southern and Northern Buddhism

SOUTHERN BUDDHISM IS ALSO CALLED THERAVĀDA BUDDHISM. Northern Buddhism Includes Sarvāstivāda and Mahāyāna Buddhism. About one hundred years after the Buddha's passing, minor differences of opinion among the Saṅgha began to emerge regarding Vinaya [monastic rules], Dhamma, and the Gautama Buddha. This caused a split of the Saṅgha into two schools: the Sthaviravāda/Theravāda and the Mahāsāṃghikas. The first schism resulted when the Mahāsāṃghikas [a group of Bhikkhus from Vagi of Vaishali] insisted that ten of the traditional rules could be relaxed a bit. They declared the new relaxed rules lawful, while the Sthaviravāda/Theravāda [the Elders] disagreed and declared them unlawful.

Subsequently, there were further schisms within the Sthaviravāda/Theravāda and the Mahāsāṃghikas. As indicated earlier, the result of these schisms was that by the 1st century B.C.E. nearly 20 different schools of Buddhism existed.

There were long-lasting schools with strong influence as well as some short-lived schools with minimal impact. At any rate, all schools possessed their own discourses. These discourses all followed the format of the Tipiṭaka – or the three baskets.

The first basket, the Vinaya Piṭaka, describes the Saṅgha's rules of conduct. The second basket, the Sutta Piṭaka, is the Gautama Buddha's teaching [Dhamma]. The third basket, the Abhidhamma Piṭaka, is a compilation of philosophical treatises of the Dhamma.

Each school had its own Tipiṭaka. Due to the difference in views among the schools, the content of each Tipiṭaka varied slightly from one another. Another layer of confusion was added with the compilation of the Abhidhamma – the writings of academic scholars who lived after the Buddha's passing.

However, by about five hundred years after the Buddha's passing, these various schools all but disappeared except for Theravāda and Sarvāstivāda. Theravāda Buddhism spread southward to Sri Lanka, Myanmar, and Thailand; Sarvāstivāda Buddhism spread northward to Kashmir, Central Asia, and China.

For four hundred years following the Buddha's passing, the Theravāda monastics of Sri Lanka recited the Buddha's Dhamma [teaching] and transmitted it orally from generation to generation. The Dhamma was finally written down officially in the latter half of the reign of King Vattagamani Abhaya of Sri Lanka [around 1st century B.C.E.]. This writing is known as Southern Buddhism's Pāli Canon or Tipiṭaka.[141]

In the north, the Sarvāstivāda monastics committed the Tri-Piṭaka to writing in Sanskrit during the reign of the third Kushan emperor, Kanishka of Yuezhi [in the early 2nd century C.E.]. Before this, the TriPiṭaka had been orally transmitted from generation to generation.

With the writing of these discourses – the Nikāyas[142] of Southern Buddhism and Āgamas[143] of Northern Buddhism – a new era began.

---

141 TriPiṭaka [Sanskrit] or Tipiṭaka [Pāli] refers to three baskets and is the term used for the three collections of the Early Buddhist discourses. It contains the Vinaya-Piṭaka, the Sutta-Piṭaka, and Abhidhamma Piṭaka.

142 Five Nikāyas: the Dīgha Nikāya [the Collection of Long Discourses], the Majihima Nikāya [the Collection of Middle-length Discourses], the Saṁyutta Nikāya [the Collection by Thematically linked Discourses], the Aṅguttara Nikāya [the Numerical Discourses], and the Khuddaka Nikāya [the Minor Collection].

143 Four Āgamas: Dīrgha Āgama, Madhyama Āgama, Saṁyukta Āgama, and Ekottara Āgama.

The Pāli language has not been used for centuries and is considered to be a dead language. Over the last two hundred years, however, Pāli has been successfully deciphered by Western linguists. Translation of the Pāli discourses into European languages began in the early 19th century. A particularly remarkable achievement is the ongoing translation by the Pāli Text Society of London, England.

In Korea, the four Nikāyas and a part of the Khuddaka Nikāya [Dhammapada, Suttanipata, and Udana] have been translated into Korean by the Center for Early Buddhist Studies and the Korea Pāli Text Society, so far. This translation is one of Korean Buddhism's most remarkable, monumental achievement in its 1,600-year history.[144] The publication of a direct translation from Pāli to Korean [which minimizes errors from indirect translations] opened a new era for Korean Buddhism.

It is assumed that the Āgama discourses of Northern Buddhism's Sarvāstivāda lasted until the 7th century C.E. and had almost the same structure of Southern Buddhism's Pāli discourses. However, nearly none of the original Āgama discourses exist today, and only part of the Mahaparinirvana Sūtra remains.

The aforementioned is only a brief history of Southern and Northern Buddhism. Now is the time for Korean Buddhists to recognize the true history of Buddhism, to listen carefully to the Buddha's authentic voice, and to humbly return to the early teaching that the Buddha presented to humanity two thousand six hundred years ago. That would be the least we could do to repay the immeasurable grace of the Buddha and the Buddha's disciples who desired to liberate those sentient beings suffering from ignorance and craving.

---

144 Buddhism was transmitted to Korea about 1,600 years ago.

— 73 —
Ven. Sayadaw U. Jotika

"Don't be busy. Get a lot of time to relax. About being busy, the Buddha said, 'not busy, living simply' [Appakicco ca sallahu-kavuttī] – busyness is the way to craziness."[145]

"The restless, busy nature of the world, this I declare is at the root of pain. Attain that composure of mind which is resting in the peace of immortality. Self is but a heap of composite qualities and its world is empty like a phantasy."[146]

Perception is compared to an incorporeal shimmering mirage in both Early and Mahāyāna Buddhism.

"Therefore, we need to discard the unwholesome perceptions and fixed ideas like ego, the great self, the true self, soul, and one mind. We need to accomplish the revulsion-dispassion-deliverance with a deep understanding that these perceptions are truly 'void, hollow, and insubstantial'[147] and ultimately are impermanent·suffering·non-self. The Buddha's true student practices by walking the path of deliverance·Nibbāna."[148]

---

145 The Snow in the Summer [Chapter 4: Life, Living and Death] by Ven. Sayadaw U. Jotika.
146 Your Best Friend and Other Essays by M.B. Werapitiya.
147 S22:95.
148 Introduction to Early Buddhism by Bhikkhu Kakmuk.

— 74 —
The Song of Enlightenment, Gungsukja of Zhèngdào gē

Penniless disciples of the Buddha say that they are poor;
They may be poor outwardly but wealthy in mind.
Although they are clothed in the rags,
Their minds possess the priceless treasures of the Path.

Without hesitation, they provide unlimited,
Priceless treasures for the benefit of all beings.
Such a mind had been perfected by
The three bodies[149] of the Buddha and
Four kinds of wisdom.
The eight kinds of liberation and
Six supernormal powers are the signs of such a mind.

A person of superior faculties understands the All at once;
A person of middle or inferior faculties cannot understand,
Despite constant perseverance.
Aha, let me keep these dirty rags in my mind only!
Why would I boast of striving so conspicuously?

Ignore slander and blame from others;
They will be tired as if they are
Trying to torch the sky with fire.

---

149 Three bodies of the Buddha [trikāya]: dhamrmakāya, Sambhogakāya, Nirmāṇakāya.

I listen to swear words as though drinking sacred nectar;
They disappear without a trace in
The inconceivable state of Nibbāna.

If I see that curse words hurled at me
Indeed have some merit,
I attain wisdom.
If I am not swayed by slander or praise,
Then, there is no need for endurance and compassion.

Because I have mastered Seon[150] and its doctrine,
The brilliance of concentration and wisdom is not
Hindered in emptiness.
What I have realized is not known to me alone;
I understand this as do all the Buddhas,
Who are as numerous as the sands of the Ganges.

The lion roars[151] the incomparable doctrine,
And upon hearing, all the minds of other animals' shatter.
Having lost its dignity, even the king's elephant raves.
Cheonnyong Palbu[152] delights upon hearing the sound.

---

150 Seon: Zen, Chan.
151 The lion's roar refers to the teaching of the Buddha.
152 Cheonnyong Palbu [eight groups of spiritual beings] are protectors of the
Buddhadharma in the Mahāyāna sūtra.

— 75 —
Muhammad and Hinduism

MUHAMMAD [571–632] IS THE FOUNDER OF ISLAM. ACCORDING to the Quran, he received a revelation from the angel Gabriel. The revelation stated that Allah is a monotheistic god who demands complete submission to him. Islam has strict rules with no distinction among monks. Islam rejects idolatry.

How many followers of Islam, who consider the Quran as the foundational doctrine, are on this earth? Every year [during the Ramadan period], millions of Muslims visit Mecca, in Saudi Arabia. This is a holy site where Muslims pray while circling the Kaaba. There are two different sects of Islam – Sunni and Shi'a. Sufism is a practice borne of Islam's contact with Persian mysticism. The famous Persian Saint and Sufi poet, Hafiz [1326–1389], was admired by the great German writer Johann Wolfgang von Goethe [1749–1832].

What about India, the birthplace of Buddhism? I recall seeing a report on January 22, 2007, about the world's largest festival, which takes place during the Indian Hindu pilgrimage Kumbh Mela. It is held every 12 years at the confluence of three rivers: the Ganges, the Yamuna, and the mythical or metaphysical "invisible" river Sarasvati [also known as the river of Wisdom]. Eight hundred million Hindus believe that during Kumbh Mela, the dates of which are determined by the Hindu almanac, the confluence [or Sangam] of these rivers becomes most sacred. They believe that by taking a bath in the rivers during the festival, all their sins are forgiven, they will be released from the cycle of rebirth, and all their wishes will come true. Twenty million people attended this festival in January of 2007.

— 76 —
"I Don't Know" and "I Wish"

THE EXPRESSIONS "I DON'T KNOW" AND "I WISH" FUEL THE END-less cycle of dependent origination. When I smell the offensive odor of the mundane world, I can be sure that the door to the supramundane lies before me. When all the mundane world seems pleasantly fragrant, I know a burning house has become my palace.

The realization of the revulsion-dispassion-destruction-deliverance-knowledge of liberation is possible when the wheel of dependent origination [the cycle of rebirth] – or the combination of cause and conditions of the "I don't know" and the "I wish" – is stopped. "I don't know" expresses ignorance. "I wish" expresses craving and clinging.

The Buddha described the mechanism to stop the cycle of dependent origination [the cycle of rebirth] as a threefold training – morality·concentration·wisdom – the Noble Eightfold Path.

In the Mahānidāna Sutta, the Buddha said the following:

> "Ānanda, it is through not understanding, not penetrating this doctrine that this generation has become like a tangled ball of string, covered as with a blight, tangled like coarse grass, unable to pass beyond states of woe, the ill destiny, ruin and the round of birth-and-death."[153]

---

153 D15.

— 77 —
The Kālāma Sutta

[BUDDHA] "Kālāmas! Do not go [accept it as truth] by oral tradition, by lineage of teaching, by hearsay, by a collection of scriptures, by logical reasoning, by inferential reasoning, by reasoned cogitation, by the acceptance of a view after pondering it, by the seeming competence [of a speaker], or because you think: 'The ascetic is our guru.'

"But when, Kālāmas, you know for yourselves: 'These things are unwholesome; these things are blameworthy; these things are censured by the wise; these things, if accepted and undertaken, lead to harm and suffering,' then you should abandon them.

"But when you know for yourselves: 'These things are wholesome; these things are blameless; these things are praised by the wise; these things, if accepted and undertaken, lead to welfare and happiness,' then you should live in accordance with them."[154]

It is likely that during the Buddha's lifetime, many different religions were practiced. According to the Buddhist discourses, there were as many as 60 different religious sects. It is reasonable to think that people then had questions about which teaching, or Dhamma, was the "right" teaching, just as they do now. The Kālāma Sutta contains the Buddha's detailed explanation about this very subject. It was given to the Kālāmas of Kesaputta in the Kingdom of Kosala.

---

154 A3:65, the Kālāma Sutta or the Kesaputtiya Sutta.

— 78 —
The Dhammapada

"A fool associating with a sage,
 Even if for a lifetime,
 Will no more perceive the Dharma
 Than a spoon will perceive the taste of soup.

"A discerning person who associates with a sage,
 Even if for a brief moment,
 Will quickly perceive the Dharma,
 As the tongue perceives the taste of soup."[155]

So, how does one become a discerning, insightful, wise person? One must strive to find the answer to the ultimate questions about "I and the world." How do we accomplish such a challenge? We must study and practice the Four Noble Truths and the Noble Eightfold Path.

---

155 Dhp. 64–65.

— 79 —
The Saṁyutta Nikāya

[Buddha] "The wise one, learned, does not feel
The pleasant and painful [mental] feeling.
This is the great difference between
The wise one and the worldling.

"For the learned one who has comprehended Dhamma,
Who clearly sees this world and the next,
Desirable things do not provoke his mind,
Toward the undesired he has no aversion.

"For him attraction and repulsion no more exist;
Both have been extinguished, brought to an end.
Having known the dust-free, sorrowless state,
The transcender of existence rightly understands."156

---

156 S36:6, the Dart Sutta.

— 80 —
The Saṁyutta Nikāya, Vedanāsaṁyutta

[BUDDHA] "When one experiences pleasure,
If one does not understand feeling
The tendency to lust is present
For one not seeing the escape from it.

"When one experiences pain,
If one does not understand feeling
The tendency to aversion [hatred] is present
For one not seeing the escape from it.

"The One of Broad Wisdom has taught
With reference to that peaceful feeling,
Neither-painful-nor-pleasant:
If one seeks delight even in this,
One is still not released from suffering.

"But when a bhikkhu who is ardent
Does not neglect clear comprehension,
Then that wise man fully understands
Feelings in their entirety.

"Having fully understood feelings,
He is taintless in this very life.
Standing in Dhamma, with the body's breakup
The knowledge-master cannot be reckoned."157

---

157 S36:3, the Abandonment Sutta.

— 81 —
Bhikkhus, Be Dreadful of Gain, Honor, and Praise

THE BUDDHA OFTEN EMPHASIZED THIS TO HIS DISCIPLES:

"Any bhikkhu who relishes and enjoys the arisen gain, honor, and praise is called a bhikkhu who has been struck with a corded harpoon, who has met with calamity and disaster, and the Evil One can do with him as he wishes. So dreadful, bhikkhus, are gain, honor, and praise, so bitter, vile obstructive to achieving the unsurpassed security from bondage. Therefore, bhikkhus, you should train yourselves thus: 'We will abandon the arisen gain, honor, and praise, and we will not let the arisen gain, honor, and praise persist obsessing our minds.' Thus should you train yourselves."[158]

Although the following happened long ago, I remember being confused about it. As a Buddhist who has taken refuge in the three jewels,[159] how should I feel about the news that a group of monastics fought among themselves, wielding wooden sticks, shoving, and barricading themselves, in a power struggle over positions within the Saṅgha?[160]

A coherent system of operation is vital to all organizations, including nations, enterprises, and Saṅghas. If the application of

---

158 S17:3.
159 The three jewels refer to the Buddha, the Dhamma, and the Saṅgha.
160 The Saṅgha [Buddhist monastic community].

the system does not meet reasonable standards or lacks objectivity, it will compromise or even bring down the entire organization. Therefore, advanced nations and societies have long recognized the importance of functional systems and have steadily developed the science of systems engineering.

However, a system is only as good as its human makers and managers. Wholesome systems come from wholesome minds and unwholesome systems come from unwholesome minds.

The more I study Buddhism, the more often I conclude that the state of the human mind determines all outcomes. The principal reason for studying Buddhism is to improve the quality of one's mind. It is undeniably true that great wisdom, mercy, and justice are a byproduct of a wholesome mind.

Peter Neujahr,[161] a Buddhist practitioner, of the Cologne Forest, Germany, is known to Koreans as a begger saint. He contributed the following article in 2003. "As the religious order grows, it must be vigilant of not creating unnecessary empty formality and vanity. In many countries, Buddhist clergy abuse the traditional lay Buddhists' faith and ignorance by having them observe the rite and ritual of the three jewels – the Buddha, the Dhamma, and the Saṅgha – accumulating wealth of the Saṅgha, enjoying the pleasure of the six senses, not observing the monastic rules, and frequently deceiving and yet being unaware of their deception. Even if the clergy does not receive the retribution of such behavior during their present lifetime, they will receive punishment after death wherever they may be in the three spheres[162] and six destinations."[163]

In Early Buddhism, the Saṅgha is one of the three jewels. It is

---

161 Peter Neujahr is known to follow the ancient Buddhist rules. He wears patched clothing, sleeps under a tree, and begs for food. He says, "The biggest joy of life is giving up the joy of ownership."

162 Three spheres: the sensuous [kama-loka], the fine-material [rupa-loka], and the immaterial [arupa-loka] sphere.

163 Six destinations: Hell, hungry ghosts, animals, asura, humans, and deva.

a community of monastics. Members of the Saṅgha, called the "noble ones" [Ariya puggala] are those who have attained the status of stream-enterer, once-returner, non-returner, and Arahant.

— 82 —
Korean Movie, "Oldboy" [Sammāvācā]

IN 2004, THE KOREAN FILM "OLDBOY" RECEIVED THE GRAND PRIZE of the Jury at the 57th Cannes Film Festival. The plot of this movie is based on the Japanese manga with the same title. After seeing this movie, I immediately became an admirer of this extraordinary film. The plot is like this: One man's irresponsible gossip – a false allegation of an incestuous relationship between siblings that involves the sister's pregnancy – spreads from person to person. The sister finally commits suicide as a result of this rumor. The brother then kidnaps the man who started the rumor and imprisons him in an underground cell for 15 years. After escaping, the man learns that his irresponsible words were to blame for his imprisonment. The movie ends with a chilling scene in which he cuts off his tongue with scissors.

In the East or the West, the importance of words cannot be overemphasized. You may pay a massive debt with well-spoken words, or you may disgrace your entire family with misspoken words.

The core teaching of Buddhism is the Noble Eightfold Path. This is an indisputable, established theory for those who study Buddhism. Any Buddhism that is not based on the Noble Eightfold Path is not the Buddhism of the Gautama Buddha.

The Gautama Buddha proclaimed that the Noble Eightfold Path is the only way to realize enlightenment. As explained in Appendix II, the Noble Eightfold Path is also called morality·concentration·wisdom or the threefold training. The components of the Noble Eightfold Path are grouped into three paths about morality, three paths about concentration, and two paths about wisdom. Morality [Sīla] refers to living a moral life. Concentration [Samādhi] refers to practicing concentration meditation. Wisdom [Paññā] refers to developing insight. Morality training requires the restraint of the five senses. Concentration training instructs us to focus the mind on one object. Wisdom training is understanding the Four Noble Truths through insight.

In the 5th century C.E., the Ven. Buddhaghoṣa wrote the Path of Purification, a treatise on Theravāda Buddhist doctrine. In it, he explained that the path to Nibbāna is found in morality·concentration·wisdom.

The morality of the threefold training includes right speech, right action, and right livelihood. Practicing right speech means abstaining from false speech, divisive speech, harsh speech, and idle chatter. The movie, "Oldboy" is a masterpiece that reveals the importance of right speech.

In fact, if one goes a little deeper in Buddhist studies, one will frequently come across the term, vocal kamma – the implicit message to be careful with words in the Buddhist discourses. The Song of Enlightenment [Zhèngdào gē], a must-read book by the monastics of the Jogye Order of Korean Buddhism, includes this statement:

> "If I deceive sentient beings with a lie, may my tongue be ripped out for as many eons as there are specks of dust and sand."

This is even eerier than the final scene of "Oldboy!"

Recently I spoke to a film director acquaintance of mine about the excellence of the movie "Oldboy." He told me that Hollywood had purchased the copyright to this movie. Maybe Hollywood thinks that society needs to be reminded of the importance of ethical speech. I told the director that he should suggest to his

Hollywood friends that they consider changing the title of the movie to "Sammāvācā" or "Right Speech," thereby using a phrase that was used two thousand six hundred years ago by the Buddha when he described the third component of the Noble Eightfold Path.

The Buddha said this about Right Speech:

"It is spoken at the proper time;
what is said is true;
it is spoken gently;
what is said is beneficial;
it is spoken with a mind of loving-kindness.

"Possessing these five factors,
speech is well spoken,
not badly spoken;
it is blameless and beyond reproach by the wise."[164]

---

164 A5.198.

— 83 —
Everlasting Poems
that Awaken Me

POEM BY BUSEOL GOESA[165]

Seeing without hindrance what is seen,
Hearing without hindrance what is heard
Lay down all discernments and quarrels . . .

POEM BY VEN. BHIKKHU MANHAE

The hills on either side of me are quiet and still,
I linger, drunk on this intoxicating scenery.
It's a little breezy but steamy hot in the temple,
The subtle fragrance of autumn
Permeates the robes of the monks.
It's still early for the fragrance of
Chrysanthemums of the South.
A former love comes to mind, vivid in my memory.
I am a mountain man
Trapped in the shadow of a wild goose,
As the moon rises above the endless autumn forest

SONG OF ENLIGHTENMENT BY VEN. BHIKKHU GYEONGHEO

When I heard of "a cow without nostrils,"
I suddenly realized enlightenment.

---

165 Goesa refers to a layman.

Then I knew that the great chiliocosm is my home.
Descending Yeonam mountain in June,
A retired man with no work to do,
Sings a song of contentment.

POEM BY VEN. BHIKKHU HYECHO

Seeing the road to my hometown in the moonlight,
I notice that the clouds move briskly across the sky.
Perhaps, I could send a letter with the clouds,
But the fast-moving wind has no interest in this plan.
My country is at the far northern end of this sky.
Here, at the western corner, I am a foreigner.
There are no geese in the sweltering south.
And so, what will fly to Guilin?

POEM BY MUJIN

Just as the hues of the setting sun
Deepen at the edge of Dongnam mountain,
My longing heart flutters when I pass this house.
I tried to forget, yet my heart cannot relinquish the memory.
The footpath between rice fields
I wander with intense longing,
As crickets chirp in the moonlight
At the ridge of Nam mountain.
I cannot erase futile events of the past by dwelling on them.
I will entrust my thoughts
To the flowing river of the Milky Way.

— 84 —
From the Avataṃsaka Sūtra

"A cow turns water into milk; a snake turns water into
poison."

This verse is from the Avataṃsaka Sūtra,[166] a Mahāyāna Buddhist discourse. This verse also appears in "the Self-Admonitions
for Beginning Practitioners," a must-read for the beginning Buddhist practitioner. This verse is followed by the prediction that if
one learns the true meaning of the verse, one will realize enlightenment. However, if one gets bogged down in literal definitions,
one will never break the cycle of birth and death [samsara].

In 1992, North Korea caused quite a stir on the Korean Peninsula when it was discovered that the nuclear reactor in Yongbyon
was processing more plutonium than it previously disclosed.
In 1994, U.S. President Bill Clinton's administration signed the
Agreed Framework with North Korea to freeze its nuclear program
in exchange for aid.

When North Korea was offered oil by the United States and
financial aid by South Korea and Japan, North Korea signed the
Nuclear Nonproliferation Treaty [NPT] in 1995. However, in 2003,
North Korea withdrew from the NPT, and the agreement to fulfill
safety regulations with the International Atomic Energy Agency
[IAEA] became a worthless piece of paper. For many years, the
incoming Bush administration tried to resolve the North Korean
nuclear problem through the six-party talks among South Korea,

---

166 Book 40, No. 12.

the United States, China, Russia, Japan, and North Korea. However, the talks became futile. At the time of this writing [2009], the 1992 nuclear issue continues to cause significant conflict and tension on the Korean Peninsula and for the international community.

For some time now, there are fools in Korea saying, "Why should the U.S. have nuclear weapons while North Korea cannot have them?" These same people also believe in a dangerous fantasy that the nuclear weapons will be South Korean's once the Korean peninsula is reunified. They are, thereby, advocating for a nuclear North Korea.

Often, misinformation is not corrected and becomes false "knowledge." It lingers in society and is eventually accepted as truth. Consider this analogy: Guns and knives, in the hands of a robber or a thief, are used as weapons to rob or steal, but in the hands of a police officer or a soldier, these weapons serve as a means to maintain safety and order in society. Likewise, there are foolish people who advocate the absurd theory that the nuclear weapons of North Korea will eventually be used for safety and order of unified Korea.

Ignorant people who are on a wrong path can be deceived by fallacious arguments and will spread unverified information. People who have blind faith are not exempt from this behavior. The Avataṃsaka Sūtra,[167] states that the study of wisdom [paññā] leads to the realization of enlightenment, while foolish teaching leads to the cycle of birth and death. This teaching of the Buddha should be pondered by all people, but especially by Buddhist practitioners.

---

167 Book 40, No.12.

— 85 —
From the Lotus Sūtra

"A ray of light illuminates
All the eighteen thousand worlds in the east,
The ground, mountains, and rivers are like
The brightness of sunlight.
This is the Buddha's exquisite Dhamma,
By all means, do not seek outward."[168]

Entering the Dhamma Sphere by Sudhanakumâra is considered the jewel of the Avataṃsaka Sūtra. In Entering the Dhamma Sphere, Sudhanakumâra meets the 53 reliable spiritual teachers to seek the Dhamma. The descriptions of these encounters unfold in an earnest and exciting manner. When Sudhanakumâra prostrated to Avalokiteśvara Bodhisattva, the 27th reliable spiritual teacher, Avalokiteśvara Bodhisattva asks, "Young monk, why are you prostrating? What are you seeking? If you are seeking the Dhamma, it is also in you." The core sūtras of Mahāyāna Buddhism – the Lotus Sūtra, the Avataṃsaka Sūtra, and the Analects of the Patriarchs – all state that the Dhamma is within oneself.

---

168 From an epigraph by the translator, Myochan, of the Lotus Sūtra.

— 86 —

The Anapanasati Sutta: Mindfulness of Breathing

"This mindfulness of breathing as a meditation subject – which is foremost among the various meditation subjects of all Buddhas, [some] Paccekabuddhas and [some] Buddhas' disciples as a basis for attaining distinction and abiding in bliss here and no ..."[169]

"Supported by the meditation subject, in-and-out breaths, one extinguishes the fire of lust, hatred, and delusion."[170]

Buddhist meditation, through the practice of body and mind, enables the realization of enlightenment. However, if you meditate to achieve a specific preconceived outcome, your meditation will not be effective. Right meditation, by definition, requires that there is no preconceived outcome.

Consider this verse in the Faithful Mind [Xìnxīn Míng] by Ven. Bhikkhu Seng-ts'an: "Forcing the mind to concentrate makes concentration even harder." This verse provides essential advice for all meditators.

---

169 Vis.VIII.155.
170 DA.iii.762.

— 87 —
From the Khuddaka Nikāya
[Udāna, Nibbāna Sutta]

[BUDDHA] "There is, bhikkhus, that base where there is no earth, no water, no fire, no air; no base consisting of the infinity of space, no base consisting of the infinity of consciousness, no base consisting of nothingness, no base consisting of neither-perception-nor-non-perception; neither this world nor another world nor both; neither sun nor moon. Here, bhikkhu, I say there is no coming, no going, no staying, no deceasing, no uprising. Not fixed, not movable, it has no support. Just this is the end of suffering.

"There is, bhikkhus, a not-born, a not-brought-to-being, a not-made, a not-conditioned. If, bhikkhus, there were no not-born, not-brought-to-being, not-made, not-conditioned, no escape would be discerned from what is born, brought-to-being, made, conditioned. But since there is a not-born, a not-brought-to-being, a not-made, a not-conditioned, therefore an escape is discerned from what is born, brought-to-being, made, conditioned."[171]

I consider the above an exclamation of the Buddha's delight.

---

171 The Nibbāna Sutta: Parinibbana (PTS: Ud 80, Ud 8.1, 8.3), translated from the Pali by John D. Ireland, the Buddhist Publication Society (BPS), Kandy, Sri Lanka 2012.

— 88 —
A Single Excellent Night Sutta

[BUDDHA] "Let not a person revive the past, or on the future build his hopes; for the past has been left behind and the future has not been reached. Instead with insight let him see each presently arisen state; let him know that and be sure of it, invincibly, unshakably. Today the effort must be made; tomorrow death may come, who knows? No bargain with Mortality can keep him and his hordes away, but one who dwells thus ardently, relentlessly, by day, by night – it is he, the Peaceful Sage has said, who has had a single excellent night."[172]

[DEVATĀ] "Those who dwell deep in the forest, peaceful, leading the holy life, eating but a single meal a day: why is their complexion so serene?"[173]

[BUDDHA] "They do not sorrow over the past, nor do they hanker for the future. They maintain themselves with what is present: hence their complexion is so serene. Through hankering for the future, through sorrowing over the past, fools dry up and wither away like a green reed cut down."[174]

---

172 M131, the A Single Excellent Night Sutta.
173 S1:10, the Forest Sutta.
174 S1:10, the Forest Sutta.

— 89 —
Material Form is Not Yours!

"THERE IS THE STORY OF THE ELDER PITAMALLA WHO, IN THE TIME he was a layman, took the pennon for wrestling in three kingdoms. ... He heard the following passage from the 'Not-yours' chapter of Scripture: 'Material form, o bhikkhus, is not yours; renounce it.' ... At the Great Minister, the Maha Vihara, at Anuradhapura, he was, in due course, given the lower ordination and the higher. ... After he had reached the state of arahantship, ... uttered this saying of joy at the final liberation from suffering:

'The world of the Fully Awakened Man, the Chief,
Holder of Right Views in all the world is this:
Give up this form, disciples; it is not yours.
Fleeting truly are component things,
Ruled by laws of growth and decay;
What is produced, to dissolution swings;
Happy it is when things at rest do stay.'"[175]

[BUDDHA] "Bhikkhus, you may well acquire that possession that is permanent, everlasting, eternal, not subject to change, and that might endure as long as eternity. But do you see any such possession, bhikkhus?" – "No, venerable sir." – " Good, bhikkhus. I too do not see any possession that is permanent, everlasting, eternal, not subject to change, and that might endure as long as eternity."[176]

---

175 The Way of Mindfulness, the Satipatthana Sutta and its Commentary by Soma Thera, the Buddhist Publication Society (BPS), Kandy, Sri Lanka 2013.
176 M22.22.

— 90 —
Truths about Birth, Aging, Illness, and Death

ONCE BIRTH OCCURS, ITS COMPANIONS – AGING, ILLNESS, AND death – come to be.

These are companions to all life. Just as two sides of a coin cannot be separated, neither can aging, illness, and death be separated from life.

A wise person who gets along well with the world – with the right perception – also accepts the companionship of aging, illness, and death.

Bhikkhu Jigwang of Nungin Meditation center once said, "The path of dying well is connected to the path of living well. One who has lived a wholesome life by the truths[177] does not need to worry about death."

Life and death are never separate. Through death, another life begins. The path of living well is directly connected to dying well, and the path of dying well is connected to the path of living well. Knowing this, I cannot emphasize enough the importance of "this life as a human."

In the last part of the Saṁyutta Nikāya is the Five Destinations Repetition Series. In this, there is a sutta about the death of human beings. It is known as the Passing Away as Humans Sutta.

"Then the Blessed One [Buddha] took up a little bit of soil in his fingernail and addressed the bhikkhus thus:

---

177 Four Noble Truths.

"What do you think, bhikkhus, which is more: the little bit of soil in my fingernail or the great earth?

"Venerable sir, the great earth is more. The little bit of soil that the Blessed One has taken up in his fingernail is trifling. Compared to the great earth, the little bit of soil that the Blessed One has taken up in his fingernail is not calculable, does not bear comparison, does not amount even to a fraction.

"So too, bhikkhus, those beings are few who, when they pass away as human beings, are reborn among human beings. But those beings are more numerous who, when they pass away as human beings, are reborn in hell. For what reason? Because, bhikkhus, they have not seen the Four Noble Truths. What Four? The noble truth of suffering, the noble truth of the origin of suffering, the noble truth of the cessation of suffering, the noble truth of the way leading to the cessation of suffering.

"Therefore, bhikkhus, an exertion should be made to understand: 'This is suffering.' An exertion should be made to understand: 'This is the origin of suffering.' An exertion should be made to understand: 'This is the cessation of suffering.' An exertion should be made to understand: 'This is the way leading to the cessation of suffering.'"[178]

---

178 S56:102.

— 91 —
Dying for One's Country

IN FRONT OF THE NEW YORK CITY HALL, THERE IS A STATUE OF Nathan Hale. He participated in the independence movement under George Washington. He was caught by British troops but refused to reveal the secrets of Washington's army. He was executed on charges of espionage. He was a new graduate of Yale University and was determined to die, if necessary, for his country. He is perhaps best known for penning this quote, in a letter sent to his sister: "I regret that I have but one life to lose for my country."

What is justice?

I define justice this way in Buddhist terms: Justice means not selling one's good conscience for profit, reverence, or fame.

— 92 —
Private First Class, Domenico "Nick" DiSalvo's Remains

I READ THE FOLLOWING IN A NEWSPAPER: ON DECEMBER 2, 1950, PFC DiSalvo, a member of the 1st Marine Division of USMC, passed away during a fierce battle at Chosin [Jhangjin] Reservoir[179] as Chinese communists overran his unit from the front, back, and middle. His remains were identified and brought back to his hometown in Ohio. He was buried with full military honors at the Ohio Western Reserve National Cemetery.

As I was reading this article, I was reminded of America's culture, which gives it the power to be a leader of the world order. America's strength lies in its ability to empower people through work. America's culture is a result of a collective consciousness that supports this ethic. America's success in world leadership is a result of mutual trust between its people and the government.

THE BATTLE OF CHOSIN RESERVOIR [THE KOREAN WAR]

By November 26, 1950, the 1st Marine Division of the U.S. Marine Corps and the U.S. Army's three Battalions of 7th Division advanced to the Kaema Plateau of South Hamgyong Province. Here they suffered a crisis of annihilation as they were encircled and attacked by the People's Volunteer 9th Army of China [of which there were seven divisions and 120,000 troops]. A brutal 17-day battle from November 26, 1950,

---

179 The Korean War [1950–1953].

to December 13, 1950, resulted in 2,500 casualties, 200 missing, and 5,000 injured. This retreat is known as one of the fiercest battles in the history of the United States. However, as a result of this retreat operation, the U.S. delayed the southward advancing of 120,000 Chinese troops and made the Hungnam evacuation possible.

In the Hungnam evacuation, 100,000 troops and 100,000 civilians were evacuated by 193 merchant ships and military transports. This was a very significant event in world history. The Hungnam evacuation was the setting of the movie "Ode to My Father" and the novel "High and Blue Ladder" by Ji Young Gong.

— 93 —
The Greatness of George C. Marshall

IN 1947, SECRETARY OF STATE GEORGE C. MARSHALL ANNOUNCED the European Recovery Program, also known as the Marshall Plan, during his commencement address to the graduating class of Harvard University. Franklin D. Roosevelt, the 32nd President of the United States, appointed Marshall Chief of Staff in 1939, although more than 30 senior generals held a rank higher than General Marshall. In 1947, then Secretary of State Marshall devised a plan which would allow recovery for Germany and other western European countries from the ashes of World War II. By designing and implementing post-war restoration aid projects, this plan decisively contributed to the revival of the European economy and prosperity. He was awarded the Nobel Peace Prize in 1953. He was the first and only career U.S. army officer to receive the Nobel Peace Prize. In promoting the prosperity of Western Europe, it could be said that the Marshall Plan helped to bring about the collapse of the Soviet Union and Central and Eastern European communist bloc countries. This ultimately allowed the West to win the Cold War.

- Secretary of War [Secretary of Defense] Henry L. Stimson who oversaw the entire Manhattan Project [Atomic Bomb Project] was a direct superior of General Marshall. Stimson said that Marshall was the most dedicated, self-sacrificing public official he had ever met.

- Britain's war hero and great politician, Winston Churchill said that Marshall accomplished the noblest endeavor in history through the Marshall Plan, which revived the European economy.
- On October 16, 1959, George C. Marshall was laid to rest in Arlington National Cemetery. He was 78 years old.

— 94 —
The Intellect of President Truman

WHENEVER I THINK ABOUT PRESIDENT HARRY S. TRUMAN, I THINK of the Korean War[180] and the military alliance that exists today between Korea and the United States.

When World War II ended in 1945 with the U.S. led coalition victory, many countries, including Korea, were liberated from colonial rule. In 1950, before the joy of liberation from 36 years of Japanese colonial rule had dissipated, Koreans faced a horrible trial. In January of that year, Stalin approved war against South Korea to Kim, Il Sung.[181] In May, Mao promised that China would get involved if the United States and the Allied forces engaged in the war. The Korean peninsula became a model of the world divided by ideology. On June 25, 1950, the new Korean government, which had been in existence for less than two years, and its people faced the North Korean invasion.

On June 24, 1950, President Truman was spending the weekend in his hometown. At 9 pm, there was a phone call for the President. It was a call made from the home of Secretary of State Dean Acheson in Maryland. Supposedly at that time, President Truman said to, "stop those bastards at any cost." It did not even take ten seconds for him to make his decision to stop the North Korean forces. He believed the Soviet Union was taking a gamble that the U.S. would not get involved in the conflict for fear that it would

---

180 Also known as 6.25 [June 25th] in Korea.
181 Kim, Il Sung was a communist dictator of North Korea [1912–1994].

launch another World War. The Soviet Union was attempting to take South Korea without repercussion.

That is why the youths of America were deployed to Korea to protect the country they did not know and people they had never met. During the Korean War [1950–1953], according to the U.S. Department of Veterans Affairs, Americans suffered greatly.[182]

Total Serving [In Theater] 1,789,000
Battle Deaths 33,739
Other Deaths [In Theater] 2,835
Other Deaths in Service [Non-Theater] 17,672
Non-mortal Woundings 103,284

The U.S. participation in the war was the result of a courageous, yet impossibly difficult decision by a great leader who could not turn away from the most sublime human values – justice, courage, and compassion.

In December 1950, British Prime Minister Clement Attlee suggested that the U.S. reconcile with the Chinese and abandon Korea. At that time, Britain had deployed two brigades to Korea. President Truman decisively rejected this suggestion! Even upon hearing the news from the battlefield that so many American youths were "falling like autumn leaves" and despite pressure from the American public for the withdrawal of troops, the Truman administration did not back down.

It has been said that President Truman was very kind to Koreans he encountered. He used to invite Korean military officers studying in the U.S. to the White House to express his support and consolation for them and Korea. In 1963 President Truman

---

182 The U.S. Department of Veterans Affairs "America's Wars."

told Kim, Jong Phil, founder of the Democratic-Republican Party in South Korea, that he regretted not reunifying Korea.[183]

It is said in both the East and the West that those who understand their history have a future. I, myself, can hardly bear to recall this dark period of Korea's history! Nevertheless, after the ceasefire on July 27, 1953, Korea adopted the American model of democracy and the market economy as its core strategy for development. Now, South Korea's economy stands firm in the international community as the 11th largest overall economy in the world.

Meanwhile, a survey of 1,016 middle and high school students conducted in 2008 on the 58th anniversary of the Korean War by the Ministry of Public Administration and Security showed that 56.8% of these Korean students did not know when the Korean War had occurred.

In May of 2005, 180 middle school students and their parents attended a lecture and memorial service that was given by those connected to the group Partisan[184] in Sunchang, Jeollabuk-do, South Korea. This service glorified the guerilla activities of this communist group.

Among those who passed the bar examination recently, some believed that the United States was the foremost enemy of South Korea.

At one annual People to People International friendship event with officers of the U.S. Eighth Army, a Korean general sitting next to me said, nowadays, six or seven out of ten recruits say the main enemy of South Korea is not North Korea, but the United States. So, I asked, "What do you do then?" He said, "Fortunately, the majority of the soldiers, through military education and training,

---

183 July 2007, Monthly Chosun, Unearthing Modern History – Truman's War by Gab Je Cho.
184 Partisan is a communist guerrilla group.

realize that their previous understanding was incorrect." I let out a long sigh of relief then.

South Korea's Defense White Paper states that South Korea and the United States are allies and that North Korea is the main enemy of South Korea.[185]

It is incredible how South Korea's education system has failed its students in making them ignorant of their history. Teachers should teach an accurate history to students! Students who are well-educated in history, and who have a variety of talents and abilities can develop curiosity and creativity to explore their unique talents.

Nowadays the majority, if not all, students are running toward the same goal of college admission. They are buried in the simplified education of acquiring test-taking skills and memorizing facts. But while this system may give students an advantage in college admission, it is limited in cultivating real intelligence. Our bleak education system holds no benefit for the future of society. Knowing facts allows one to remember and recall accumulated information, but only the intelligence to process information gives one the means to solve problems creatively.

Today, our society needs talented people with a full range of intelligence from all corners of society. Many share the sentiment that in Korea, only students from top universities, ones with family wealth, connections, and influence can prosper. This must change. We need to encourage students to cultivate the wisdom to be masters of their lives, and not to only accumulate the knowledge of facts. A person with genuine intelligence, who

---

185 The white paper is published once every two years to inform the Korean public of defense policies and future policy direction. According to the Defense White Paper published by the Korean government on January 16, 2019, North Korea is no longer an enemy of South Korea.

is generous to neighbors, charitable, appreciative, and possesses a wholesome character should be the role model in our society.

Walkerhill Hotel is located in Gwangjang-dong, Seoul, South Korea. Camp Walker is a US military base in Daegu, South Korea. These were named after General Walker, commanding general of the U.S. Eighth Army.

At the beginning of the Korean War, the North Korean army rapidly advanced. General Walker held the North Korean army at the Nakdong River. Supposedly, he told his troops that he would defend South Korea even if it cost him his life. There were seven battles from the night of August 18, 1950, to August 23, 1950. The great military leader, Korean General Paik, Seon Yup, was also involved in this military action, during which 2,300 South Korean troops and 1,282 U.S. troops were killed. The North Korean forces suffered 5,690 deaths.

The Nakdong River defensive line was held through these fierce battles and provided a foothold for General MacArthur to accomplish the miraculous Incheon Landing Operation. At dawn on September 15, 1950, under the command of General MacArthur, 70,000 troops from eight countries, on 261 ships[186] including aircraft carriers, destroyers, and cruisers defied all odds by making a successful landing.

General Walker was on his way to Uijeongbu for a front-line inspection in December 1950. On this trip, at the age of 61, he passed away in a traffic accident when his jeep collided with a vehicle of the South Korean army. How many young Koreans know about this?

Koreans must forever remember and be deeply grateful to President Truman, a great leader who have shown justice, courage, and compassion. They must also not forget the sacrifice General

---

186 Total 261 ships: 225 U.S., 12 UK, 3 Canada, 2 Australia, 2 New Zealand, 1 Netherlands, 1 France, 15 Korea.

Walton Harris Walker made, when he held the Nakdong River defensive line, thereby enabling the successful Incheon Landing Operation of General MacArthur.

Sages of ancient times said that the most useless human being in the world is one who does not know gratitude. A nation that does not remember its history is destined to be ruined. How do Koreans remember the grim 518 years during the Chosun Dynasty, a tributary nation to the Qing Dynasty of China for 258 years? Do Koreans remember being a colony of Japan for 36 years? Do they even remember the Korean War?

In May 2008, there were protests against imported beef from the United States. As a result, Gwanghwamun street in Seoul was under siege by demonstrators for two months. Then the Korean government seemed to recognize the hasty nature of its decision to import the U.S. beef and decided to renegotiate its position to resolve the issue. This resulted in another group with a hidden agenda inciting the public in "Opposition to the Import of American Beef." This group opposes democracy and the democratic government; they are anti-American. They promote boycotts of certain media outlets they do not like, even going so far as to take illegal possession of media buildings and commit violence and destruction.

When the authority of the government is undermined, the nation's very existence is threatened. I worry that the activist culture – hanging banners, waving flags, lighting candles, frequently exercising violent acts, clashing with the government – is being adopted by Koreans today. Ideological confrontation can bring unforeseen and devastating consequences to a nation.

While the sublime human value is compassion, it must not supersede justice. Therefore, leaders must be virtuous. For the sake of justice, a leader needs the courage to be selfless. Most people desire a strong leader who is just and courageous.

To those who are holding a candlelight vigil on Gwanghwamun

street in front of the Seoul City Hall, how about lighting a candle in the hope that young minds will be filled with the wisdom to imagine a future for the world, understood through the lens of history.

The law of cause and effect is the core of Buddhist teaching. Anaxagoras, a Greek philosopher [510 B.C.E.–428 B.C.E.], said that no matter how the universe evolved, the law of cause and effect is the unchanging truth. We need to respect the law of kamma.

"OUR NATION HONORS

HER SONS AND DAUGHTERS

WHO ANSWERED THE CALL

TO DEFEND A COUNTRY

THEY NEVER KNEW

AND A PEOPLE

THEY NEVER MET

1950·KOREA·1953"

The above inscription is etched on the Korean War Veterans Memorial in the National Mall, Washington, D.C.

2009 is the 56th anniversary of the Korean War Armistice. The U.S. Senate and the U.S. House of Representatives unanimously passed the "Korean War Veterans Recognition Act" and designated July 27th as National Korean War Veterans Armistice Day. The U.S. flag was flown half-staff on July 27th from 2000 to 2003. Each year since then, the U.S. government encourages the display of the flag on July 27th.

This law was enacted in part due to the persistent effort of Hannah Kim. She was a 25-year-old Korean-American graduate student, who, in 2008, worked on a project called "Remember 727." She made phone calls to nearly 10,000 people for this project. At times, she would be exhausted and discouraged, but she reminded herself of what Margaret Mead, the American cultural anthropologist, said: "Never doubt that a small group of thoughtful, committed citizens can change the world; indeed, it's the only thing that ever has." I thank Ms. Hannah for her work on "Remember 727," commemorating the Armistice Agreement. I wish her and her organization the best for their future endeavors.[187]

---

187 Critical points in the timeline of events leading up to the Korean War, presented in documents by Russian President Boris Yeltsin to President Kim, Young Sam of South Korea in 1994.
· March 5, 1949: Stalin meets with Kim Il-sung. Kim Il-sung inquires about Soviet leadership's views on the reunification of the Korean peninsula by force.
· August 14, 1949: Kim Il-sung expresses the need to attack South Korea to the Soviet Ambassador to North Korea, Terentii Shtykov.
· April 1950: Stalin meets with Kim Il-sung. Stalin agrees to North Korean's reunification plan.
· May 14, 1950: Stalin sends a telegram to Mao Zedong indicating his approval of the North Korean proposal "to move toward reunification."
· May 15, 1950: Mao Zedong agrees with North Korea's three-tiered attack plan of South Korea.
· June 12, 1950: The North Korean army advances to within ten–15 km north of the 38th parallel.
· June 25, 1950: The official start of the Korean War.
· July 5, 1950: China promises to enter the war, with Stalin providing air protection, should the Allied forces cross the 38th parallel.
· September 29, 1950: Following the Incheon Landing Operation by the allied forces, Kim, Il Sung sends a letter to Russia requesting China's direct intervention.

— 95 —
Courageous Leaders and Emasculated Leaders

THE DATE OF JUNE 4, 1989 MARKS ANOTHER STAIN ON HUMAN history – the Tiananmen Square Massacre in China. Ordinary citizens who demanded democracy – which I consider a legitimate human right – were brutally massacred. According to unofficial news sources, there were reports of 5,000 deaths and 30,000 injured in the Tiananmen Square Massacre.

On the 20th anniversary of the Tiananmen Square Massacre, the U.S. Secretary of State Hillary Clinton said that China "should examine openly the darker events of its past and provide a public accounting of those killed, detained or missing, both to learn and to heal."

Many Buddhists in South Korea would like to invite the Dalai Lama, who is known as "the apostle of peace" worldwide, to South Korea. But the South Korean government has prevented this from happening out of fear of upsetting China.

Such response of the government reveals the shortsightedness and weakness of its leader. Although there might be immediate minor political benefits from taking such a stance, it does not help the nation or its citizens at all in the long run.

What value is there to living a little more prosperously, but as a coward? It is much more forward-thinking and worthwhile to live a just life. Is there any value to be a human without having a sense of justice, courage, and compassion? My position, although perhaps extreme, is that such humans are no better than living corpses.

In 2002, the U.S. President, George W. Bush gave the following speech at Tsinghua University, China: "My country certainly has its share of problems, no question about that. And we have our faults. Like most nations, we're on a long journey toward achieving our own ideals of equality and justice. Yet there's a reason our nation shines as a beacon of hope and opportunity, a reason many throughout the world dream of coming to America. It's because we're a free nation, where men and women have the opportunity to achieve their dreams. No matter your background or your circumstance of birth, in America you can get a good education, you can start your own business, you can raise a family, you can worship freely, and help elect the leaders of your community and your country. You can support the policies of our government, or you're free to openly disagree with them. Those who fear freedom sometimes argue it could lead to chaos, but it does not, because freedom means more than 'every man for himself.'"[188]

President Reagan visited West Berlin on June 12, 1987, and made the following speech at the Brandenburg Gate, looking at the Berlin Wall, "Mr. Gorbachev! Tear down this wall." Several staffers and aides advised against this verbiage, saying it was too extreme. Nevertheless, President Reagan liked the passage and decided to keep it. The Berlin Wall came down about two years and three months later, on November 9, 1989. President Reagan's courage and foresight shined.

I admire these dignified responses from courageous leaders of the United States, which is a leader of the International Order.

A just person has no fear. Courage and compassion always accompany a just person. A coward has a lot of anxiety. A coward has no courage because of his or her fear of self-diminishment.

Do we want to live as living corpses, devoid of justice, courage, and compassion? Every day, we have the opportunity to make

---

188 https://georgewbush-whitehouse.archives.gov/news/releases/2002/02 /20020222.html.

a choice to live a life of justice, courage, and compassion – the sublimated value of human beings.

> There is a cool wind in the late autumn,
> Falling leaves are blowing in the wind.
> A farewell is promised with every encounter,
> Passing away is guaranteed with anything that arises.
> Today, the color of impermanence is deepening.[189]

---

189 Mujin.

— 96 —
Mature Ethical Awareness
of the Japanese

JAPAN STARTED THE PACIFIC WAR BUT WAS DEFEATED AS A RESULT of the atomic bombings of Hiroshima and Nagasaki on August 6, 1945, and August 9, 1945, respectively. After the War, in a little over half a century, Japan emerged as the third largest economic power in the world. To what can we attribute the economic recovery and success of Japan?

It is widely known that most Japanese are honest, modest, and considerate of others. I attribute Japan's success to the mature and ethical collective consciousness – deeply rooted in the honesty, diligence, frugality, and consideration for others – of most Japanese people.

If the goal of American education is to "grow up and gain independence from your parents," the Japanese model is, "Honesty is most important. Be diligent and frugal, and do not be a burden on others under any circumstance."

Japan is a quiet country. It is not quiet due to a lack of problems. However, when they have a problem, they do their utmost to find a solution, and to make sure that nothing is overlooked in setting up a system to prevent similar problems in the future. A difference of opinion is resolved in private. Due to excellent problem-solving skills in private, the Japanese always seem calm!

The culture of a country is characterized by the collective consciousness of its citizens. The rise and fall of any nation is dependent on the state of the collective consciousness of its citizens. In other words, the maturity of moral consciousness is key to the rise and fall of a nation.

Let's put a spotlight on some of Japan's historical facts, beginning nearly a century before the defeat of Japan in the Pacific War. In 1868, Japan opened a new chapter in its history called the Meiji Restoration. During this period, practical imperial rule was restored to the Empire of Japan under Emperor Meiji when three nobles initiated a bloodless coup that ended the rule of the Tokugawa shogunate. Saigō Takamori of Kagoshima was the leader of this coup, and he is still admired by many Japanese today.

At this time, Fukuzawa Yukichi, a gifted educator and reformist thinker, immerged. His portrait can be found on the 10,000-Yen banknote of Japan today. He established Japan's first private school, Keio-Gijuku which developed into Keio University, one of Japan's prestigious private universities. Through his publications – An Encouragement of Learning [学問のすすめ Gakumon no Susume], An Outline of a Theory of Civilization [文明論之概略 Bunmeiron no Gairyaku], and articles in Jiji-Shinpo [a newspaper he started in 1882] – he advocated for international independence and the establishment of a nation-state by cultivating a spirit of independence and self-respect in the Japanese people.

He spread the philosophy of "Datsu-A Ron [脱亞入歐]" into Japanese politics. This philosophy advocated that Japan abandon the declining Chinese culture [Chinese literature and Confucianism] and emulate western civilization as soon as possible. He stoked the fire of the "paradigm shift" of modernizing Japan. This movement of embracing western values resulted in the construction of a railway between Tokyo and Yokohama. This railway was built by the Japanese with the help of English technology in 1872 [the 5th year of Meiji Restoration]. By 1900 over 7,000 kilometers of the railway had been constructed throughout Japan. Thus, began the history of Japan's railway, which is rated one of the best railways in the world today.

The Sino-Japanese War began in 1894, and by 1895, Japan

claimed victory. Ten years later, in 1904, Japan was embroiled in the Russo-Japanese War.

At that time, Russia had a 4.5-million-man army, compared to Japan's total force of 850,000. Despite this, the Russian Baltic fleet under the command of Admiral Rozhdestvensky was almost destroyed by the Japanese fleet led by Togo Heihachiro in the Battle of Tsushima Strait. Japan's victory in this battle led to the Treaty of Portsmouth which was signed on September 5, 1905, between Russia and Japan. This Treaty ceded the southern half of Sakhalin to Japan. Japan was again victorious.

With Japan's advancement of imperialism, it declared war on the United States on December 7, 1941, by conducting a surprise military attack on the U.S. Pacific Fleet at Pearl Harbor. The U.S. military suffered 3,435 casualties and loss of or severe damage to 188 planes, eight battleships, three light cruisers, and four miscellaneous vessels.[190]

On June 5, 1942, Japan attacked the United States forces on Midway Atoll. Although the U.S. won the Battle of Midway, both nations suffered significant losses. One reason for this U.S. victory is that American cryptographers were able to determine the date and location of the planned Japanese attack. It is also speculated that a conflict between the Japanese army and navy – competition for excessive loyalty to the Japanese Emperor – led to the Japanese defeat at Midway.

This planet we inhabit – the earth – is an ecosystem. What is an ecosystem? It is a community of organisms, interacting with each other and their physical environment. In an ecosystem, all living things must consume other living things to stay alive. This is the fate of all things in ecosystems. Perhaps this is why we humans cannot avoid wars. Regardless, the history of wars leaves us with a clear lesson that we must choose our politicians and leaders wisely.

---

190 U.S. Government National Archives.

The culture of a nation or society is a product of the collective consciousness of its constituents. Wholesome consciousness results in wholesome culture, unwholesome consciousness results in unwholesome culture.

Our national leaders or local advocates are elected by the people, each of which has his or her own political view. When the overall population lacks wholesome political views, an unwholesome outcome is inevitable. Examples of unwholesome leadership include:

- Japan's Hideki Tojo, who started the Pacific War
- Germany's Adolph Hitler, who is responsible for World War II and the Holocaust
- The Soviet Union's Joseph Stalin, who purged many hundreds of thousands and sent more than a million of the Russian population to forced labor camps in the name of Communist revolution
- North Korea's Kim, Il Sung who started the Korean War
- North Korea's Kim, Jong Il, a dictator addicted to the illusion of heroism, even while millions of his constituents starve

There are two distinguishing features of war criminals such as these. One, they do not value human life. The other is that they are talented in clouding and deceiving the minds of the population. When an entire population ignores unwholesome behaviors – such as dishonest talk to protect one's profit or to mask inequalities, indifference to those in desperate social circumstances, and self-absorption leading to distorted individualism – these behaviors become social norms. These populations enable unfit leaders to become popular and ultimately suffer the catastrophic consequences of their own making.

In a mature democracy, the population can prevent national disasters or misfortunes through a system of checks and balances.

Today, at this moment, our thoughts, words, and actions that arise with our consciousness have direct and indirect effects on ourselves, our neighbors, and society. This is the law of cause and effect of Buddhism.

Buddhist practice begins with the following moral tenets:

Abstain from false, divisive, harsh speech, and idle chatter
Abstain from the destruction of life
Abstain from taking what is not given
Abstain from sexual misconduct
Abstain from intoxicating drinks and drugs
Earn one's living by a right livelihood

So, even in discussing the right Buddhist practice and enlightenment, we must always mindfully practice this morality. Without doing so would be like making a mirror by grinding a roof tile or cooking rice by steaming sand.

— 97 —
Saigō Takamori's Outlook on Life

UNDERSTANDING THE BUDDHIST CULTURE OF JAPAN WILL NATU-rally lead to a gradual understanding of the culture of Japanese society. I think that the Japanese people have a deep interest and exceptional talent in literature. The ethical awareness of the Japanese – that the value of human life must be based on ethics and morality – is an underlying theme in Japanese poetry, songs, and novels.

This culture becomes the driving force behind its national patriotism whenever Japan finds itself in conflict. During the Pacific War, parents held back their tears as they told their children going off to serve Japan that they needed to be willing to die for their country and their emperor. Since time immemorial, it seems that Japanese people shared an understanding that ethics and morality are the driving force behind the advancement of Japan as a nation, as well as the sublimated value of individuals, themselves.

It is from this culture that Yasunari Kawabata won the Nobel Prize for Literature for the *Snow Country* in 1968. And in 1994 the Nobel Prize in Literature was awarded to Kenzaburo Oe, of whom the literature committee of the Swedish Academy said, "with poetic force [Oe] creates an imagined world, where life and myth condense to form a disconcerting picture of the human predicament today."

In Japan, many great literary awards attract the attention of the Japanese people. Observing the Japanese reading quietly in crowded trams, one can witness the level of appreciation the Japanese people have for literature.

One of the popular sayings by the Japanese goes, "Which mountain is the highest among the mountains in Japan? Of course, it is Mount Fuji. Who is the most important person in Japanese history? It is Saigō Takamori."

So, who is Saigō Takamori [1828–1877], that the Japanese love and honor? Let's take a brief look at his life. It is presumed that he favored a very "simple" life. The word "simple" here has an implied meaning that he was a courageous and straightforward person who even transcended the fear of death.

One day, faced with the sudden death of his Daimyo [lord] and tough political prospects, he decided to follow the ancient practice of junshi.[191] However, his friend, Gesshō[192] convinced him not to follow through with junshi. Instead, he and his friend fled to Saigō's hometown, Satsuma.[193] However, upon finding out that his friend would not be protected in Satsuma, and indeed, executed if captured, the two friends threw themselves into Kagoshima Bay. Only Gesshō drowned, and Saigō narrowly escaped from death. Saigō thought deeply about the fact that he could not end his life despite his wish to do so. He believed that there must be a reason for him to live and to perform his divine calling.

Saigō Takamori was born to a samurai clan of Kagoshima in 1828. Although of modest means, members of his family were honorable warriors that served the feudal lord Daimyo, as the royal guards. Saigō possessed the spirit and virtue of a samurai – he was caring, humble, courageous, tolerant, and possessed excellent swordsmanship skills. He had many colleagues and great flocks of followers. His temperament intensified with his education.

---

191 Junshi is the ancient practice that a servant commits suicide after a lord's death.

192 Gesshō [1813–1858] was the chief Buddhist monk of Kyoto temple.

193 Satsuma is a town in Satsuma District, Kagoshima Prefecture, Japan.

He studied Zen Buddhism and the Chinese philosopher Wang Yang-ming's teaching about the unity of knowledge and action. His motto was to "revere heaven and love people."

Saigō was one of the three core leaders of the Meiji Restoration that overthrew the Tokugawa Shogunate. Saigō became a commander of the army of the Satsuma-han which was stationed in the Imperial capital, Kyoto. In the summer of 1871, Saigō was promoted to the first army chief of the new Japanese government. However, he resigned later that year after losing a debate over a military expedition to Korea for which he had been advocating. He returned to his home in Kagoshima, where he spent his time farming and hunting.

While staying in his hometown as a commoner, the Japanese government proposed to purchase the land in Tokyo which Saigō owned. When he asked why the government needed the land, he was told that they wanted to build the Bank of Japan on it. Saigō immediately gifted the property to the government for this purpose. At the end of the Tokugawa Shogunate era, the government awarded land to many warriors who participated in the Imperial restoration to start commerce.

Less than ten years after the Meiji Restoration, Saigō was leading a rebellion against the new government he previously helped to form. On September 24, 1877, the government forces carried out the last attack on Kagoshima where Saigō was during the Satsuma Rebellion. Although exact details regarding Saigō's death are unknown, his subordinates claim that Saigō asked a faithful lieutenant to assist him in his suicide by cutting off his head. He was 49. During this conflict, 6,840 government troops and 6,400 troops under Saigō's command were killed.

Saigō has been called the "last samurai" because he retained his traditional values in a society that was becoming more and more modern. Just 12 years after his failed rebellion, he was pardoned by the Meiji government, and in 1898 a famous statue of Saigō and his dog was erected in Tokyo's Ueno Park.

Although there will be various viewpoints and controversies among historians about Saigō, he exemplifies one who went a step further, transcending life and death with extreme straightforwardness and righteousness. The way Saigō ended his life may have even put an end to future conflicts and disputes among samurais. Today, nearly a century and a half after his death, he remains a popular historical and cultural icon. He symbolizes Yamato-damashii – the spirit of Japanese people. He is known for unifying Japan.

In Satsuma, where he was born and lived, a giant statue of him was built to honor him. The statue stands in Gionnosu park, named after Jetavana Vihara of India [Kosala Kingdom], which is known as the place where the Buddha stayed most frequently.

"Do not deal with the human but deal with heaven.
One who will become great must deal with heaven.
Do your best, and do not blame others
But blame yourself for not giving your best."[194]

I have been intrigued by the life of Saigō Takamori for many years. My thoughts about him in this essay are based on the many stories I've read over the years about him in books, newspapers, magazines and websites.

---

194 Saigō Takamori.

— 98 —
Maple Leaves by Thomas Bailey Aldrich

"OCTOBER turned my maple's leaves to gold;
The most are gone now; here and there one lingers:
Soon these will slip from out the twigs' weak hold,
Like coins between a dying miser's fingers."[195]

Let's get ready for winter before winter comes. Although my body is sound today, will it be sound tomorrow? No matter how tightly I grasp life, it will eventually slip through my fingers. It seems that the poet takes to heart the example of the falling maple leaves, suggesting that life should be lived without fuss or attachment.

---

195 Thomas Bailey Aldrich.

— 99 —
Four Great Men of England

WHEN I THINK OF ENGLAND, I AM REMINDED OF FOUR GREAT MEN.

The first is T.W. Rhys Davids [1843–1922] who founded the Pāli Text Society in 1881, and who also played a pivotal role in translating the Pāli Suttas – the Buddha's authentic voice – to English.

The second is William Shakespeare [1564–1616], one of the greatest English writers, who wrote about truth and the impermanent nature of the world in a most poetic way.

Third, I think of Sir Winston Leonard Spencer Churchill [1874–1965], a war hero and a recipient of the Nobel Prize in Literature [1953]. He was perhaps the most prominent political leader in England's history. England fought in World War I and II. During World War I [1914–1918], England suffered 512,600 casualties, with an additional 1,528,500 wounded. There were 223,600 prisoners of war on the Western Front alone.[196] The total worldwide casualties from World War II [1939–1945] exceeded 50 million. On May 10, 1940, Winston Churchill became Prime Minister. When he met his Cabinet on May 13, 1940, he told them that "I have nothing to offer but blood, toil, tears, and sweat."[197] At age 90 he died and is now considered a war hero. The 2002 BBC production, "100 Greatest Britons" was based on a television poll conducted to determine whom the United Kingdom public considered the greatest Brit-

---

196 The World War I Databook by John Ellis & Michael Cox, P. 270.
197 Winstonchurchill.org.

ish people in history. Winston Churchill overtook Newton and Shakespeare as the greatest Briton in history.[198]

Fourth on my list of great British men is Dr. Alexander Fleming [1881–1955] who received the Nobel Prize in Physiology in 1945 for the discovery of Penicillin. In the summer of 1928, while in his London laboratory Dr. Fleming was studying the common staphylococcal bacteria known to cause boils. Dr. Fleming had just gone on a two-week vacation. While he was gone, he had accidentally forgotten to store the petri dish with a staphylococcus culture in the incubator. Upon his return, he noticed that a blue mold grew on this culture and that the staphylococcus bacteria next to the mold had been completely dissolved. This indicated to him that a certain substance produced by the fungus exhibited a strong antimicrobial action. Since the fungus belonged to the genus Penicillium, the substance was named Penicillin. Since Dr. Fleming's initial discovery of Penicillin, which is effective against bacterial infections, more advanced antibiotics have been developed, increasing human life expectancy.

198 www.geni.com/projects/100-Greatest-Britons-BBC-Poll-2002.

— 100 —

Law of Kamma is the Core of Buddhism

BEING ABLE TO HELP OTHERS BRINGS ME JOY. HOWEVER, THERE
is no need to dwell on the thought that I helped someone. My
actions are known to the entire universe; therefore, dwelling on
my accomplishments is self-serving and pointless.

Because the law of kamma is the truth, blessings are for those
with a selfless attitude.

Wholesome encounters are within
The kamma of wholesome encounters,
Unwholesome encounters are within
The kamma of unwholesome encounters.
Who gives and who receives,
When all are arising within me?[199]

Noting her desire for sensual pleasures, Elder Bhikkhuni
Uppalavaṇṇā attained Arahantship and said,

"Sensual pleasures are like spears and darts,
A Bundle of aggregates is like a guillotine.
What you call 'delightful,'
Is now a 'non-delight' to me."[200]

---

199 Mujin.
200 Therigatha [Book of Verses of Elder Bhikkhunis] 234, translated by Nancy
Acord.

— IOI —

Let It Go

Do not grab on to anything, either mental or material.
Let it go.
Only then will you be at peace,
Since you have nothing to lose.
Do your best in what you need to do,
But do not do it with the expectation of reward.
Without expectations,
Good deeds and the profits you accumulate will be yours.[201]

If you let go a little, you will have a little happiness.
If you let go a lot, you will have a lot of happiness.
If you let go completely, you will be free.[202]

There are three meditation methods described in the Early
Buddhist teaching: mindfulness, concentration, and insight meditation. Mindfulness has two key components: awareness and clear
comprehension, and is the foundation of both concentration
and insight meditation. Generally speaking, all three meditation
methods involve being exclusively aware of the meditation subject and letting all other phenomena fall away. Through persistent
practice of insight meditation, one can deconstruct the meditation subject; at this point one becomes aware of the "arising and

---

201 Mujin.
202 Ven. Ajahn Chah.

passing away of dhamma"[203] and the cause and condition of such phenomena. Insight meditation allows one to know and see the true or ultimate reality of oneself and the world. This process is essential in the attainment of deliverance·Nibbāna.

When one is released from the fetters of lust – the desire of possession, a delusion caused by the inversion of perception, mind, and view[204] – one lives a life of freedom. Buddhist meditation acts like a beacon that guides a ship in the darkness of the night. Buddhism is perfect teaching that resolves human suffering. Why does the desire of possession lead to suffering? Because at the moment, we think we own an object [including our bodies!], that object owns us. Contrarily, non-possession means we are not owned by any object. More specifically, when we know that every object [including our body] is empty and there is nothing we can claim ownership of, revulsion and dispassion arise, lust is extinguished, and suffering ends.

"Knowing and seeing the reality as it is" [emptiness] is the fundamental subject and core of Buddhist meditation. It is stated in many places in Buddhist discourses that we can be freed from lust, hatred, and delusion through meditation. Nibbāna is achieved when the hot flame of the "three poisons" [lust, hatred, and delusion] have been extinguished.

---

203 The dhamma, as in all phenomena [sabbe-dhamma], is the basic component that makes up all phenomena. In the Abhidhamma, it is defined as 'an ultimate component, with its own unique character, that cannot be deconstructed further.' (DhsA.39 Etc.) The dhamma as the smallest component is called the ultimate reality [paramattha dhamma].
204 A4:49.

102

The Five Aggregates Lack Substantial Self

Does my body exist?
Yes, it does.
Why do I say it does?
It exists because
It is governed by dependent origination.

Does my body not exist?
No, it does not.
Why do I say it does not?
It does not exist because
It is governed by dependent origination.[205]

From the standpoint of Buddhism, human beings are the five aggregates,[206] acting together and interdependently.

Human suffering can be divided into two categories: physical and mental suffering. Physical [material] suffering can be caused by illness, due to bacterial or viral infections, an imbalance of the biosystems, aging body parts, impaired bodily function, etc. Typically, medication is used to treat physical pain. Mental suffering is different. There are various causes of mental suffering. Fundamentally, however, mental suffering arises from our clinging

---

205 Mujin.
206 Mentality [feeling, perception, mental formation, and consciousness] and Materiality [body, material form].

to the delusion – due to the inversion of perception, mind, and view – that the self possesses the five aggregates.

Despite Korean Buddhism's 1,600-year history and regardless of what the Heart Sūtra said about the five aggregates being empty and indeed not the self, many Korean Buddhists insist that the self exists. Again, this delusion is caused by the inversion of perception, mind, and view and is the cause of suffering. The Gautama Buddha said the remedy for this ignorance was meditation. We must meditate to overcome "ignorance" and find "wisdom."

So, the core of Buddhism includes meditation practice. Understanding Buddhism without practicing meditation is like trying to use a cart with a missing wheel. This is specifically explained in the Buddha's teaching.

In ignorance, the five aggregates become I,
Out of ignorance, the five aggregates are not I.
In ignorance, life and death is my destiny,
Out of ignorance, life and death is
A dream within a dream.[207]

---

207 Mujin.

103

About the Path and Dhamma, the Core of Buddhism

WHAT IS THE PURPOSE OF STUDYING AND PRACTICING BUDDHISM? It is to escape the despair and suffering of life caused by birth, aging, illness, and death. This gloomy reality of life applies to all of us without exception. If there is no way to avoid this, happiness becomes unobtainable.

Although I know the purpose of studying and practicing Buddhism, my day to day life does not always reflect this. I find myself chasing, breathlessly, after things and experiences that will feed my sensual pleasure, not knowing whether I am living or dying, and clinging drunkenly on the sensual pleasure that arises and passes away momentarily. Is it too much to say that this pretty much describes my life in general?

No matter which way I analyze my life, I come to the conclusion that "living" is accompanied by "dying." Perhaps this is what Shakespeare meant when he wrote in one of his sonnets: "So shall thou feed on Death, that feeds on men."[208]

The Buddha addresses this as well when he referred to those who confuse momentary sensual pleasure with true happiness, all the while ignoring the crucial issue of life and death.

Desire hunger for pleasure, pleasure hunger for desire.
The Buddha commands us to stop

---

208 Shakespeare sonnet 146.

The pursuit of desire for sensual pleasure;
This is the logical conclusion of the Four Noble Truths.
We must thoroughly observe this
Spectacular magical phenomenon with insight.
Our impulse to use the mind without mindfulness
Is the cause of all suffering.[209]

As I stated previously, to fully comprehend Buddhism, one only needs to understand the Four Noble Truths correctly. This is sometimes called "right understanding." In other words, the essence of the Buddha's teaching is explained in the Four Noble Truths. The path, or practice, of this teaching, is fully explained in the Noble Eightfold Path.[210] The Four Noble Truths and the Noble Eightfold Path are the official formulae and core of the Buddha's teaching.

Although Chinese Seon Buddhism has been heavily influenced by Chinese culture, Korean Buddhists, due to misunderstanding, have considered Chinese Seon Buddhism to authentically represent Buddhism. Addiction to Chinese Seon Buddhism is serious among Korean Buddhists. However, Seon Buddhism is only one of many Buddhist traditions. Even Seon Buddhism has five major schools and seven sects. Ganhwa Seon, which uses hwadu as the meditation subject, is one of these schools. Based solely on the assertion by Ganhwa Seon, many Korean Buddhist monastics and their followers state without hesitation that Ganhwa Seon is the best practice to realize enlightenment.

Those who practice Mantra Seon within Pure Land Buddhism – one of many denominations of Buddhism – may insist that Mantra Seon is the best practice; those who practice Esoteric Buddhism may insist recitation of mantra like "Om Mani Padme Hum" is the best practice.

---

209 Mujin.
210 The Noble Eightfold Path is sometimes referred to as the middle path.

As a practitioner of Early Buddhism – fundamental and authentic teaching of the Gautama Buddha – it is impossible for me to accept such claims and propaganda of the aforementioned various Buddhist sects. However, I do understand that there was a natural progression of the development of Buddhism over the last two thousand six hundred years, involving practitioners from vast territories with different races, nationalities, languages, native religions, and culture.

The history of Mahāyāna Buddhism, which appeared around four to five hundred years after the passing of the Buddha, shows that Mahāyāna Buddhists edited and published new versions of Mahāyāna discourses themselves. The Lotus Sūtra belongs to the first group of the newly edited discourses. At the beginning of the Lotus Sūtra, it is stated that it is the best discourse among all discourses.

About four hundred years later, or about eight to nine hundred years after the passing of the Buddha, the Flower Ornament Sūtra or Avatamsaka Sūtra – a beautiful Buddhist novel – was compiled in Khotan.[211] The Flower Ornament Sūtra claims itself to be the best discourse among all discourses.

We must note here the critical fact that no matter who has claimed this or that theory about the Buddha's teaching, such a theory cannot supplant the Buddha's own authority. When it comes to enlightenment, the Gautama Buddha is the undeniable authority.

By declaring one's own theory or method to be the best in realizing enlightenment, one essentially glorifies oneself above the Gautama Buddha. We must always question the theories of such people! One must approach the Buddha's teaching with humility.

In his book *Recorded Sayings of Linji*, the Ven. Bhikkhu Linji – the founder of the Linji school of Chinese Chan Buddhism – stated, "Make yourself a master wherever you are, then where you

---

211 Khotan is a Buddhist kingdom that lasted 1,000 years in Central Asia.

are now is the true place." He also said, "Now is the right time to do; if not, there would be no other right time." My understanding of these two phrases is that we must maintain awareness [sati] and clear comprehension [Sampajañña] continuously without interruption. This thought correlates to the practice of mindfulness, the core theory of Early Buddhism. Ven. Bhikkhu Linji is asking that we stay awake, at this very moment wherever we are. He warns us not to be confused by ontological concepts that are empty and but a mirage.

As I ponder the meaning of these phrases by the Ven. Bhikkhu Linji, I wonder how much I really understand the true meaning of the author. It reminds me of the lecture by Dr. Edward Kim, my teacher, at Changwon National University in 1996. He quoted Hon. Dalai Lama's statement, "Be careful of words, the meaning of words, and the human experience of the speaker." I wholeheartedly agree with the Hon. Dalai Lama's words. I think it is essential that one needs to approach words, even by the most respected teachers, with care to avoid misunderstanding or misinterpretation of the true meaning of the author.

My good friend, Prof. Kim, Sang Hyun of Dongguk University spent his career studying Ven. Wonhyo. He told me a quote by Wonhyo, which further reinforced my conviction about knowing one's own limitation in understanding any other's work. Wonhyo said, "a bird flying high up, sees how low the mountains are, and flying over the ocean, sees the narrowness of the stream."

The eternal questions of human beings about the universe and the self are being addressed through 21st-century cutting-edge science and advanced mathematics that are sometimes beyond our imagination. I feel that as this happens, there is more and more common ground discovered between science and Buddhism.

The Buddha explained his teaching using the scientific methods: observing [of conventional reality], questioning [through research], theorizing [making hypotheses], practicing [through experimentation], reviewing [noting results], and confirming [reaching a conclusion]. Through the understanding of Buddhism, we may know the reason for suffering caused by the endless cycle of rebirth. Because of the compassion, blood, sweat, and tears of the noble ones who eagerly sought to preserve the Buddha's teaching, and for those pioneers who translated and dispensed the Buddha's teaching to many, the means for enlightenment shines upon the human race of the 21st century like a rising sun from the East.

In the Visuddhimaga [the Path of Purification] – an indisputable commentary of Abhidhamma of Early Buddhism – the author, Ven. Bhikkhu Buddhaghosa explained the meaning of "purification" as follows:

"Herein, purification should be understood as Nibbāna, which is devoid of all stains, is utterly pure. The Path of Purification is the path to that purification; it is the means of an approach that is called the path."[212] He explained the meaning of the Path of Purification five ways, as they appear in various suttas.[213] This explanation is followed by a comment that the Path of Purification requires morality·concentration·wisdom. In short, the Path of Purification provides a guide to obtaining Nibbāna.

The Buddha said that sentient beings endlessly endure the painful cycle of rebirth because of the fetters caused by our inversion of perception, mind, and view. He listed ten fetters[214] that must be removed to gain the ultimate happiness, Nibbāna.

These fetters can be unlocked with one key, only. That key is the Noble Eightfold Path, which integrates morality·concentration·wisdom. One realizes the path and the fruit of Sotāpanna when fetters one, two, and three are removed. Next, one real-

---

212 Vis.I.5.

213 Vis.I.6.

214 The ten fetters: self-view, attachment to moral precepts and religious ritual, doubt about the Buddha, Dhamma, Saṅgha, precepts, dependent origination, etc., sensual lust, ill will, attachment to the form spheres, attachment to the formless spheres, conceit, restlessness, and ignorance.

izes Sakadāgāmi after fetters one, two, and three have been removed and when fetters four and five are weakened. One realizes Anāgāmi when the first five fetters are completely removed. One becomes an Arahant when all ten fetters are removed.

In the Diamond Sūtra, the ten fetters are grouped into two groups: the five lower fetters and the five upper fetters. The noble ones are mentioned repeatedly as Sotāpanna, Sakadāgāmi, Anāgāmi, and Arahant in the Diamond Sūtra. The "four pairs or the eight noble ones"[215] are Sotāpanna – the stream-enterer, Sakadāgāmi – the once-returner, Anāgāmi – the non-returner, and Arahant, the one who triumphs over enemies.

Taking a closer look at the ten fetters, it is clear that there is hope for us. The Buddha said that one achieves the path and the fruit of Sotāpanna by removing the first three fetters. By attaining the path and the fruit of Sotāpanna, one can realize enlightenment within seven lifetimes. And the only key to unlock these fetters is the Noble Eightfold Path. Therefore, it cannot be emphasized enough that a proper understanding and practice of the Noble Eightfold Path – the middle path – is essential in Buddhism.

---

215 The path of Sotāpanna, Sakadāgāmi, Anāgāmi, and Arahant; the fruit of Sotāpanna, Sakadāgāmi, Anāgāmi, and Arahant. Therefore, it is called four [Sotāpanna, Sakadāgāmi, Anāgāmi, and Arahant] pairs [path and fruit] or eight [4+4] noble ones.

— 104 —
All Conditioned Phenomena are Impermanent – A Hwadu of Great Mystery

THERE ARE FIVE MAJOR SCHOOLS AND SEVEN SECTS IN CHINESE Chan [Seon] Buddhism. Ven. Bhikkhu Dahui Zonggao [1089–1163] from the Yanqi sect of the Linji school advocated Ganwha Seon. There are over 1,700 kinds of hwadus[216] [gongans] in Ganhwa Seon.

Early on, when I first became interested in Buddhism, I realized that before reaching the stages of Sotāpanna, Sakadāgāmi, Anāgāmi, and Arahant, I should consider all phenomena of the [conventional] world to be nothing but hwadus. My rationale was that "knowing" in conventional reality is not "knowing" through the "right view" but mere conceptual knowing. This is common knowledge to those who study Buddhism. Therefore, all phenomena of the world have to be hwadus for ordinary Buddhists.

Perhaps, that is why Ven. Bodhidharma – the transmitter of Chan [Seon] Buddhism to China – answered, "I don't know" to emperor Wudi's question, "Who are you?"

Anyone who is born is subject to aging, illness, and death; this is not the "right view" but a delusion that belongs to conventional reality. The Gautama Buddha realized this truth.

When we remove these fetters – rooted in ignorance – by walk-

---

216 Hwadu, a meditation subject, is also known as the great question, doubt, or gong-an and used in the Ganhwa Seon which is the principal type of meditation practiced in contemporary Korean Buddhism.

ing the Noble Eightfold Path, the right view will become known to us. In the Diamond Sūtra, it is stated that all outer appearances are impermanent. Therefore, if one knows that appearance is not real, one knows the Buddha [Tathāgata].

— 105 —
The Mundane and the Supramundane

One who is tied to the fetters of the concept
Is called a sentient being,
One who has removed the fetters of the concept
Is called a noble one.
The sphere of the concept is called the mundane,
Beyond the sphere of the concept is the supramundane.
But there is no separate mundane and supramundane.
These are only manifestations of sentient beings.[217]

The "concept" above arises through the six sensory faculties, the six sense objects, and the six sense consciousnesses. Through mindfulness and insight, the concept is deconstructed. This is the core of Buddhist meditation practice.

The 18 elements[218] enable us to construct the conceptual sphere. The fetters that bind us to the concept can be removed by developing the right awareness [Sammāsati], clear comprehension [Sampajañña], and wisdom [Vipassanā]. The concrete instructions for removing the fetters are delineated in the Noble Eightfold Path.

One can obtain the path and the fruit of Sotāpanna, Sakadāgāmi, Anāgāmi, and Arahant through the Noble Eightfold Path.

---

217 Mujin.
218 The six sensory faculties, the six sense objects, and the six sense consciousnesses are also known as the 18 elements.

The Buddha called these practitioners who have removed fetters the noble ones.[219]

What is the teaching of the Diamond Sūtra of Mahāyāna Buddhism? The world of conditioned phenomena [the conceptual, conventional world] is as fleeting as a dream, a phantom, a water bubble, a shadow, dew, or a lightning bolt. One must break free from the play of the perception. This is the teaching of the Diamond Sūtra.

It is stated in the prologue of *Demian*, a novel by Nobel Prize author Hermann Hesse, that "The bird fights its way out of the egg. The egg is his world." The egg is also my world – nothing but a conceptual world based on my perception!

The Buddha teaches us in many suttas that our actions define us. One day, "While the brahmin students Vāseṭṭha and Bhāradvāja were walking and wandering for exercise, this discussion arose between them: 'How is one a brahmin?'" After disputing about this question, they ended up asking the Buddha the same question. The Buddha gave them a clear definition of a brahmin. The Buddha said, "I call him not a brahmin because of his origin and lineage … One is not a brahmin by birth, nor by birth a non-brahmin. By action is one a brahmin, by action is one a non-brahmin … Asceticism, the holy life, self-control and inner training – by this one becomes a brahmin, in this supreme brahminhood lies … One possessing the triple knowledge, peaceful, with being all destroyed: know him thus, O Vāseṭṭha, as Brahmā and Sakka for those who understand."[220]

> There is no coming or going in ultimate reality,
> There is coming or going in conventional reality.
> For the noble one who attained ultimate reality,
> Ultimate reality is the conventional reality and
> Conventional reality is the ultimate reality.

---

219 Having removed the first three fetters through the tenth fetter, one is called a noble.
220 M98, the Vāseṭṭha Sutta.

There is no life or death in ultimate reality,
There exists life and death in conventional reality.
For the noble one who attained ultimate reality,
Life and death exist and do not exist.[221]

The truth of the mundane is conditioned; the truth of the supramundane is unconditioned. When one cuts off craving and removes the ten fetters, ignorance will disappear. Then, coming and going, conventional and ultimate reality, life and death, the mundane and supramundane are a dream within a dream.

---

221 Mujin.

— 106 —

Selecting an Appropriate Type of Meditation is Important

IN THE BRAHMIN UṆṆĀBHA SUTTA, THE BUDDHA SAID TO THE Brahmin Uṇṇābha that these five faculties: eye, ear, nose, tongue, and body take recourse in the mind; the mind takes recourse in mindfulness; mindfulness takes recourse in deliverance; deliverance takes recourse in Nibbāna.[222]

The subject of mindfulness is the "I." Therefore, being mindful of phenomena that occur within the concept of the "I" is important. What is outside of the "I" is not meaningful. Why? Because the "I" attains deliverance·Nibbāna. The Buddha said in the Digha Nikāya, "And being thus unattached he has experienced for himself[223] perfect peace."[224] The Mahāsatipaṭṭāna Discourse states that the subjects of mindfulness are broadly grouped into the body, feeling, mind, and mental objects. These subjects are further divided into 14 kinds of body, nine kinds of feeling, 16 kinds of mind, and five kinds of mental objects. There are 44 subjects in total. The Buddha instructs us to select one subject from these 44 subjects and to remain mindful of the subject.

The key components[225] of mindfulness meditation are the

---

222 S48:42.
223 "He has experienced for himself" means he experienced by and within himself according to the commentary (DA.ii.527).
224 D1:1.36.
225 Key components of mindfulness are lucid awareness [sati] and clear comprehension [Sampajañña].

foundation of the two types of meditation in Early Buddhism. One is concentration meditation [Samatha], and the other is insight meditation [Vipassanā]. In the Path of Purification, there are 40 meditation subjects suggested for concentration meditation. By concentrating on one of 40 meditation subjects, one creates a learning sign [uggaha-nimitta] and a counterpart sign [paṭibhāga-nimitta]. By concentrating on the counterpart sign, one attains absorption-concentration [appanā-samādhi, Jhāna]. Vipassanā is a practice of seeing, with insight, one of the 71 ultimate realities [paramattha dhamma] that are further classified as mind, mental factors, and materiality. When one sees the dhamma with insight, impermanence, suffering, and non-self can be clearly understood.

> "Bhikkhus, when anyone has not developed and cultivated mindfulness of the body, Māra[226] finds an opportunity and a support in him."[227]

---

226 Māra refers to the demon associated with death, rebirth, and craving; all forces that hinder deliverance·Nibbāna.
227 M119.23.

— 107 —

An Apple Tree, A Petri Dish, the Nature of Light, and the Buddha's Quest

CURIOSITY CAN CHANGE THE COURSE OF HUMANITY.

Sir Isaac Newton [1642–1927] observed an apple falling from a tree and wondered why the apple always fell straight down. This question inspired him to develop his theory of universal gravitation, which in turn opened up new horizons for science.

In 1928, Dr. Fleming [1881–1955], a British microbiologist, noticed an unusual phenomenon on a petri dish of a staphylococcus culture while studying the common staphylococcal bacteria. The blue mold grew on the petri dish while the staphylococcus bacteria around the mold had completely dissolved. This discovery led to the development of Penicillin, which protects humans from germs and viruses. He received the Nobel Prize in Physiology and Medicine in 1945. From Penicillin, more advanced antibiotics that increased the average life expectancy of humans have been developed.

Einstein, the father of modern physics, had many questions about light. He wondered about the nature of the brightness of the light. He questioned if he could see himself in the mirror if he traveled close to the speed of light. By pursuing answers to these questions, he eventually received the Nobel Prize in Physics in 1921 for his discovery of the law of the photoelectric effect. His theory of relativity fused time and space into spacetime. $E = MC^2$

is perhaps the most famous equation in the world. In this equation Einstein revealed the relationship between energy and mass.

Two thousand six hundred years ago, the Gautama Buddha wondered why humans, once born, must age, become ill, and die. In order to find the answer to this question, he relinquished his status as a prince destined to inherit his father's kingdom, and left home at the age of 29. After six years of extremely harsh practice, he found a clear answer to this question. The Buddha obtained his answer utilizing three [number 4,5,6] of the six supernormal powers.[228]

The detailed explanation of the answer to the Buddha's original, fundamental question is called Dhamma, the Buddha's teaching. It is possible for human beings to be freed from the pain of birth, aging, illness, and death through Dhamma.

The Buddha said the following in the Udana Sutta:[229]

"Then, on realizing the significance of that, the Blessed One [Buddha] on that occasion exclaimed:

There is, monks, an unborn – unbecome – unmade – unfabricated. If there were not that unborn – unbecome – unmade – unfabricated, there would not be the case that escape from the born – become – made – fabricated would be discerned. But precisely because there is an unborn – unbecome – unmade – unfabricated, escape from the born – become – made – fabricated is discerned."

---

228 The following six supernormal powers are developed based on the fourth jhāna.
   1. Knowledge of supernormal psychic powers [iddhividha-nāṇa].
   2. Knowledge of the divine ear [dibbasota-nāṇa].
   3. Knowledge of the penetration of the minds of others [cetopariya-nāṇa].
   4. Knowledge of the recollection of former lives [pubbenivāsa-anussati-nāṇa].
   5. Knowledge of the divine eye [dibbacakkhu-nāṇa].
   6. Knowledge of the destruction of the taints [āsavakkhaya-nāṇa].
229 Ud 8.3, the Nibbāna Sutta: Unbinding.

This said, it is possible to end the suffering, caused by birth and death. If so, where is our hometown that we must return to? We must return to the sphere that transcends "the world of birth and death" – spacetime. Birth and death cannot occur where time does not exist. No space means no here and no there; therefore, I am omnipresent. When the drape of ignorance is lifted, there is here and here is there . . .

Upon learning that his closest friend, Michele Besso had passed away, Einstein said, "Now he has departed from this strange world a little ahead of me. That means nothing. People like us, who believe in physics, know that the distinction between past, present and future is only a stubbornly persistent illusion."

— 108 —

Mujin's Journey as a Buddhist

A sailor on a boat constructed from the five aggregates,
Rowing the four rough oceans![230]

May my speech, action, and livelihood
Be full of compassion.

May I not engage in useless
Lust, hatred, or delusion.

May I only travel on the wholesome path,
Leading to enlightenment.

May I keep on traveling this wholesome path,
Even when I encounter the hardships of life,
Without being conquered or intimidated by them.

May I know and see the Dhamma one day,
Before the boat sinks.

May I attain the path and the fruit.

Mahāprajñāpāramitā, Mahāprajñāpāramitā,
Mahāprajñāpāramitā[231]

---

230 The oceans in the four cardinal directions around Mount Sumeru.
231 Mahāprajñāpāramitā: The great perfection of wisdom.

— Appendix 1 —
The Illusion of Feeling, the Poison of Stress, and Meditation: the Wisdom of Life

LONG AGO, I READ THIS QUOTE SOMEWHERE, "THE DUST STORM, kicked up by so many pursuing the illusion of feeling, blocks the sun." Indeed, I can relate to that.

About two thousand six hundred years ago, the Gautama Buddha, a great teacher of humans and devas, told us that we must clearly understand the illusory nature of feeling; then we can be free from suffering. This teaching appears many times in Early Buddhist Suttas [discourses]. The Buddha taught us detailed explanations about feeling in the Connected Discourses on Feeling.[232] This Pāli Sutta has been translated into English by Nyanaponika Thera[233] of Germany who became a monk in Sri Lanka. In turn, this English version was translated into Korean by Bhikkhuni Daerim,[234] the head of the Center for Early Buddhist Studies. I have read the Korean version by Bhikkhuni Daerim many times.

---

232 S36.
233 Nyanaponika Thera [1904–1994] was co-founder of the Buddhist Publication Society, contemporary author of numerous seminal Theravāda books, and teacher of contemporary Western Buddhist leaders such as Bhikkhu Bodhi.
234 Bhikkhuni Daerim [1962–] is the head of the Center for Early Buddhist Studies, studied Sanskrit, Pāli, and the Prakrits languages in India, Sri Lanka, and Myanmar for 13 Years. She translated Nikāyas and other Theravāda books from Pāli to Korean.

The preface of *Contemplation of Feeling* by Nyanaponika Thera starts like this, "'To feel is everything!' – so exclaimed a German poet. These are rather exuberant words, and they do point to the fact that feeling is a key factor in human life. Whether people are fully aware of it or not, their lives are chiefly spent in an unceasing endeavor to increase their pleasant feelings and to avoid unpleasant feelings. All human ambition and striving serve that purpose: from the simple joys of a humdrum existence to the power urge of the mighty and the creative joy of the great artist. All that is wanted is to have more and more of pleasant feelings, because they bring with them emotional satisfaction, called happiness."[235]

Most people run after sources of pleasant feelings their entire life. In doing so, however, they are not aware that they become the slaves of such sources, suffering greatly until death.

The Gautama Buddha defined three forms of the poison in human beings: lust, hatred, and delusion. Lust arises when one tries to obtain things that give one pleasure and joy. Hatred arises when one tries to avoid things that give one displeasure and suffering. Delusion arises when one feels neither pleasure nor pain.

Let me explain further about the true nature of feeling by referencing the Feeling [Vedana] Sutta.[236] The feelings rooted in the three poisons – lust, hatred, delusion – become the cause and condition of craving [Taṇhā] for those who are addicted to them. Craving eventually leads to suffering – birth, aging, illness, death, union with what is displeasing, separation from what is pleasing, not getting what one wants, and the five aggregates subject to clinging. In doing so, we are forced to endure the endless cycle of rebirth. To become free of suffering, we must clearly see the true nature of feeling – impermanence, suffering, and non-self.

According to a joint study conducted over several years by the

---

235 "Contemplation of Feeling: The Discourse-Grouping on the Feelings," translated from the Pali, with an Introduction by Nyanaponika Thera.
236 S36.

Johns Hopkins Medical School and the Toronto Medical School, stress is one of the contributors to the acceleration of human aging and disease. Stress is an important issue in modern life. I was studying and gaining a greater understanding of the Pāli Suttas when I came across this study. I thought the finding of this study was significant.

I consider stress to be a manifestation of hatred. We call any unpleasant feeling that arises – whether from a displeasing encounter, the loss of something pleasing, or the frustration of not getting what we want – stress. There are two kinds of stress: eustress [positive stress] and distress [negative stress]. The stress I'm referring to is distress.

But why would stress accelerate human aging and cause disease? Our body that works interdependently with the mind [mentality] is very complex and delicate. The human body's endocrine system has many glands: the hypothalamus, pituitary, parathyroid, adrenals, pineal body, reproductive organs, and pancreas. These glands secrete hormones which play essential roles: some affect metabolism, some keep the internal environment of bodily fluid constant, some promote physical growth, some regulate developmental conditions, some promote sexual maturity or help us maintain a sexual rhythm, some are involved in the reproductive process, some help in healing wounds, and some control energy production.

Our state of mind can influence our hormones. Pleasant, unpleasant, or neutral feelings affect hormone secretion levels. For instance, when a person is experiencing hatred, hormones such as adrenaline, cortisol, etc., are secreted by the endocrine organs. These hormones can be harmful to one's body. Although scientific studies are sparse on this subject, meditation supposedly increases beneficial hormones such as serotonin, DHEA, GABA [gamma aminobutyric acid], endorphins, GH [growth hormone], and melatonin, and decreases cortisol.

The meditation method taught by the Gautama Buddha is an

excellent tool that can be used to overcome the stress of hectic modern living and bring us happiness and peace of mind.

The Gautama Buddha taught his followers to abandon hatred. When one abandons hatred, one can sleep better and reduce or eliminate unpleasant feelings. This is not easy to achieve, but wouldn't we all be happier to sleep peacefully without worries, sadness, anger, etc.? To have peace and happiness, one must strive to develop the maturity to avoid engaging in hatred regardless of the situation.

The Early Buddhist suttas consist of five Nikāyas [volumes]. Of these five, the Khuddaka Nikāya contains many short stories. In Dhammapada, which is one of the books belonging to the Khuddaka Nikāya, it is repeatedly emphasized that the most terrible poison is hatred. Trivial matters can trigger such hatred in people! Hate does not help solve problems. Hatred only poisons our minds and encourages us to commit unwholesome deeds. It ruins our health by secreting stress hormones. Therefore, shouldn't it be our priority to eliminate the cause of stress? The Buddha told his followers to check their progress of practice by measuring hatred within themselves.

[A CERTAIN BHIKKHU] "Then a certain bhikkhu approached the Blessed One, paid homage to him, sat down to one side, and said to him: 'Venerable sir, what now is feeling? What is the origin of feeling? What is the way leading to the origination of feeling? What is the cessation of feeling? What is the way leading to the cessation of feeling? What is the gratification in feeling? What is the danger? What is the escape?'

[BUDDHA] "'There are, bhikkhu, these three feelings: pleasant feeling, painful feeling, neither-painful-nor-pleasant feeling. This is called feeling. With the arising of contact there is the arising of feeling. Craving is the way leading to the origination of feeling. With the cessation of contact there is the cessation of feeling. This Noble Eightfold Path is the way leading to the cessation of feeling; that is, right view ... right concentration.

"The pleasure and joy that arise in dependence on feeling: this is the gratification in feeling. That feeling is impermanent, suffering, and subject to change: this is the danger in feeling. The removal and abandonment of desire and lust for feeling: this is the escape from feeling.'"[237]

I often had conversations with old Bhikkhu Kyung Bong of Gukrak[238] Hermitage. He said, "I remind people who are hurriedly running after the illusion of feeling that there are 24 hours in a day. If we work for nine hours, sleep for eight hours, and play for four hours, we would still have three hours left in the day. Therefore, I recommend to people that they meditate quietly for at least 30 minutes to an hour out of that remaining three hours, every day."

If one cannot exhale, one's life is over. If one cannot inhale, one's life is also over. Therefore, the continuity of our lives is connected to the continuity of inhaling and exhaling. In meditation, one clearly knows one's in-and-out breaths.

[BUDDHA] "Breathing in long, he knows: 'I breathe in long'; or breathing out long, he knows: 'I breathe out long.' Breathing in short, he knows: 'I breathe in short'; or breathing out short, he knows: 'I breathe out short.' He trains thus: 'Experiencing the whole body,[239] I will breathe in'; he trains thus: 'Experiencing the whole body, I will breathe out.' He trains thus: 'Tranquillizing the bodily formation, I will breathe in'; he trains thus: 'Tranquillizing the bodily formation, I will breathe out.'"[240]

---

237 S36:23.
238 Heaven, Paradise.
239 The body means the breath.
240 S54.

Meditation is one of the most valuable practices in human life. It leads to the treasure trove of true happiness. It is a secret that only those who practice it know. The Gautama Buddha told us that only those who practice meditation would know the true nature of reality, would transcend this world, and end their suffering.

The Buddha taught us meditation, showing us the way to cultivate the wisdom to escape from the poison of stress and to avoid feelings rooted in ignorance. We can follow the Path of Purification through meditation.

[BUDDHA] "Bhikkhus, when mindfulness of breathing is developed and cultivated, it is of great fruit and great benefit. When mindfulness of breathing is developed and cultivated, it fulfils the four foundations of mindfulness. When the four foundations of mindfulness are developed and cultivated, they fulfil the seven enlightenment factors. When the seven enlightenment factors are developed and cultivated, they fulfil true knowledge and deliverance."[241]

---

241 M118.

— Appendix 11 —
Path to Deliverance·Nibbāna: the Four Noble Truths and the Noble Eightfold Path

AFTER SIX YEARS OF EXTREMELY INTENSE PRACTICE, THE GAU-tama Buddha realized enlightenment under the bodhi tree. He came to know and see the ultimate reality of the universe. How-ever, the Buddha said, "So too, bhikkhus, the things I have directly known but have not taught you are numerous, while the things I have taught you are few. And why, bhikkhus, have I not taught those many things? Because they are unbeneficial, irrelevant to the fundamentals of the holy life, and do not lead to revulsion, to dispassion, to cessation, to peace, to direct knowledge, to deliverance, to Nibbāna. Therefore, I have not taught them."[242]

What did the Buddha teach? He said, "And what, bhikkhus, have I taught? I have taught: 'This is suffering'; I have taught: 'This is the origin of suffering'; I have taught: 'This is the cessation of suffering'; I have taught: 'This is the way leading to the cessation of suffering.' And why, bhikkhus, have I taught this? Because this is beneficial, relevant to the fundamentals of the holy life, and leads to revulsion, to dispassion, to cessation, to peace, to direct knowledge, to deliverance, to Nibbāna. Therefore, I have taught this."[243]

---

242 S56:31.
243 S56:31.

The Gautama Buddha taught that through the Four Noble Truths, one could end the suffering of endless rebirth [which is rooted in ignorance] and attain deliverance·Nibbāna. This is the totality of the Buddha's teaching. Therefore, a proper understanding of Buddhism means understanding the Four Noble Truths. The right practice which leads to wisdom, will arise from the correct understanding of the Four Noble Truths.

Now, let's take a closer look at the Four Noble Truths.

First Truth: The Noble Truth of Suffering [dukkha ariya-sacca]

There are many religions in the world. A claim they all share is that while human beings are subject to suffering in varying degrees, their brand of faith can offer a solution and eliminate suffering. So too, Buddhism offers an elaborate description of the many kinds of human sufferings and a solution to end suffering:

> [BUDDHA] "Now this, bhikkhus, is the noble truth of suffering: birth is suffering, aging is suffering, illness is suffering, death is suffering; union with what is displeasing is suffering; separation from what is pleasing is suffering; not to get what one wants is suffering; in brief, the five aggregates subject to clinging are suffering."[244]

> [JAMBUKHĀDAKA] "Friend Sāriputta, it is said, 'suffering, suffering.' What now is suffering?

> [SĀRIPUTTA] "There are, friend, these three kinds of suffering: suffering due to pain, suffering due to change, suffering due to formations. These are the three kinds of suffering."[245]

I suppose that if there is no suffering in the world, there wouldn't be any need for religion. And if that day comes, would it be that ultimate reality [unconditioned] becomes known to all? The truth is that once birth occurs, we are tied to the links

---

244 S56:11, the Setting in Motion the Wheel of the Dhamma Discourse.
245 S38:14, the Suffering Discourse.

of dependent origination [origin of suffering, anuloma] and we cannot avoid suffering.

Second Truth: The Noble Truth of the Origin of Suffering [dukkha-samudaya ariya-sacca]

If the first truth is about the unavoidable nature of human suffering, the Noble Truth of the Origin of Suffering is about craving, the cause of suffering, which is rooted in ignorance.

Third Truth: The Noble Truth of the Cessation of Suffering [dukkha-nirodha ariya-sacca]

If the second truth is about craving, the cause of suffering, the Noble Truth of the Cessation of Suffering is about removing the cause of suffering, craving.

Fourth Truth: The Noble Truth of the Way Leading to the Cessation of Suffering [dukkha-nirodha-gāmini-paṭipadā ariya-sacca]

If the third truth is about removing the cause of suffering, the Noble Truth of the Way Leading to the Cessation of Suffering offers a path to accomplish this. That path is the Noble Eightfold Path.

The Buddha told us what to do with suffering – define it, understand its origin, and know that it must be stopped. Then he actually prescribed a way for us to end suffering.

The Buddha said, "And what, monks, is the Noble Truth of the Way Leading to the Cessation of Suffering? It is just this Noble Eightfold Path, namely: – Right View, Right Thought, Right Speech, Right Action, Right Livelihood, Right Effort, Right Mindfulness, Right Concentration."[246]

So, the Noble Eightfold Path is the path that leads to the cessation of suffering, the fourth truth of the Four Noble Truths. This is also called the middle path because it avoids either extreme of sensual pleasure or the self-mortification of asceticism. When

---

246 D22:21.

the Buddha discovered that these two extremes do not help us reach enlightenment he abandoned them and chose, instead, the middle path. This is described in the Setting in Motion the Wheel of the Dhamma Sutta.[247]

This middle path opens one's eyes, allowing wisdom to arise, and shows the ultimate reality, which leads to Nibbāna. The Noble Eightfold Path is the core of the Buddha's 45 years of teaching. Through the practice of this path, one can understand its profound meaning, and eventually reach the shore of Nibbāna.

Let's review the Buddha's teaching of the Noble Eightfold Path in the Mahāsatipaṭṭhāna Sutta: The Greater Discourse on the Foundations of Mindfulness:

> [BUDDHA] "'And what, monks, is the Noble Truth of the Way Leading to the Cessation of Suffering? It is just this Noble Eightfold Path, namely: – Right View, Right Thought[248], Right Speech, Right Action, Right Livelihood, Right Effort, Right Mindfulness, Right Concentration.
>
> "And what, monks, is Right View? It is, monks, the knowledge of suffering, the knowledge of the origin of suffering, the knowledge of the cessation of suffering, and the knowledge of the way leading to the cessation of suffering. This is called Right View.
>
> "And what, monks, is Right Thought? The thought of renunciation, the thought of non-ill-will, the thought of harmlessness. This, monks, is called Right Thought.
>
> "And what, monks, is Right Speech? Refraining from lying, refraining from slander, refraining from harsh speech, refraining from frivolous speech. This is called Right Speech.

---

247 S56:11.
248 Alternate translation of Right Thought: Right Intention.

"And what, monks, is Right Action? Refraining from taking life, refraining from taking what is not given, refraining from sexual misconduct. This is called Right Action.

"And what, monks, is Right Livelihood? Here, monks, the Ariyan disciple, having given up wrong livelihood, keeps himself by right livelihood.[249]

"And what, monks, is Right Effort? Here, monks, a monk rouses his will, makes an effort, stirs up energy, exerts his mind and strives to prevent the arising of unarisen evil unwholesome mental states. He rouses his will ... and strives to overcome evil unwholesome mental states that have arisen. He rouses his will ... and strives to produce unarisen wholesome mental states. He rouses his will, makes an effort, stirs up energy, exerts his mind and strives to maintain wholesome mental states that have arisen, not to let them fade away, to bring them to greater growth, to the full perfection of development. This is called Right Effort.

"And what, monks, is Right Mindfulness? Here, monks, a monk abides contemplating body as body, ardent, clearly aware and mindful, having put aside hankering and fretting for the world; he abides contemplating feelings as feelings ... ; he abides contemplating mind as mind ... ; he abides contemplating mind-objects as mind-objects, ardent, clearly aware and mindful, having put aside hankering and fretting for the world. This is called Right Mindfulness.

"And what, monks, is Right Concentration? Here, a monk, detached from sense-desires, detached from unwholesome mental states, enters and remains in the first jhāna, which is with thinking and pondering, born of detachment, filled with delight and joy. And with the subsiding of thinking and

---

249 D22:21.

pondering, by gaining inner tranquillity and oneness of mind, he enters and remains in the second jhāna, which is without thinking and pondering, born of concentration, filled with delight and joy. And with the fading away of delight, remaining imperturbable, mindful and clearly aware, he experiences in himself the joy of which the Noble Ones say: 'Happy is he who dwells with equanimity and mindfulness', he enters the third jhāna. And, having given up pleasure and pain, and with the disappearance of former gladness and sadness, he enters and remains in the fourth jhāna, which is beyond pleasure and pain, and purified by equanimity and mindfulness. This is called Right Concentration. And that, monks, is called the way of practice leading to the cessation of suffering."[250]

There are specific references in the Samyutta Nikāya regarding the Noble Eightfold Path:

[BUDDHA] "The destruction of lust, the destruction of hatred, the destruction of delusion: this is called the Deathless. This Noble Eightfold Path is the path leading to the Deathless;[251]

"It is in this way, bhikkhus, that a bhikkhu with a rightly directed view, with a rightly directed development of the path, pierces ignorance, arouses true knowledge, and realizes Nibbāna.[252]

"Those who have undertaken the Noble Eightfold Path have undertaken the noble path leading to the complete destruction of suffering.[253]

"Bhikkhus, these eight things, when developed and cultivated, lead to going beyond from the near shore to the far shore."[254]

---

250 D22:21.
251 S45:7.
252 S45:9.
253 S45:33.
254 S45:34.

By practicing the Noble Eightfold Path, we can eradicate ignorance – the root cause of suffering – and attain deliverance·Nibbāna. From the first moment of our existence, we suffer. This suffering is described in many ways.[255]

The Noble Eightfold Path can be grouped into three subjects: morality·concentration·wisdom. It is also called "unsurpassed perfect enlightenment" [anuttarā sammā saṃbodhi]. The Gautama Buddha realized the cycle of rebirth and law of kamma through the Four Noble Truths and the Noble Eightfold Path. He said, "Destroyed is birth, the holy life has been lived, what had to be done has been done, there is no more for this state of being."[256]

A life rooted in ignorance necessitates that the cycle of rebirth will continue. Although there is no inherent "I," some still cling to the notion that "I exist." These people become subject to the cycle of rebirth. When ignorance is uprooted, one will have an understanding of the non-self, and such knowledge will lead to the cessation of rebirth and suffering. Rooted in ignorance, only sentient beings experience the cycle of rebirth; there is no rebirth for the Arahant.

From the unknowable beginning, lust, hatred, and delusion rooted in ignorance have bound sentient beings to the cycle of rebirth. One can remove lust, hatred, and delusion through wisdom and end the cycle of rebirth, and hence, suffering.

With the right understanding of Buddhism, one will gain the right view of self and the world, thus becoming honest, helpful, and compassionate. For someone who sees self and the world with the right view, worry, anxiety, fear, and lamentation will have no foothold anywhere, anytime. This is the foundation of

---

255 The four kinds of suffering are birth, aging, illness, and death; the eight kinds of suffering are the previous four kinds of suffering plus the following four kinds of suffering: union with what is displeasing, separation from what is pleasing, not to get what one wants, and the five aggregates subject to clinging.
256 S35.

the great deliverance·Nibbāna. The path to deliverance·Nibbāna is carefully explained in the Noble Eightfold Path. Responsibility of the practice of the Noble Eightfold Path lays entirely upon us individually.

The importance of the Noble Eightfold Path is related in this reference to the Buddha's past lives in the Mahāgovinda Sutta: The Great Steward of Digha Nikāya:

[PAÑCASIKHA] "Do you remember this, Lord?'

[BUDDHA] "'I do, Pañcasikha. At that time I was the Brahmin, the Great Steward, and I taught those disciples the path to union with the Brahmā-world.' 'However, Pañcasikha, that holy life does not lead to disenchantment, to dispassion, to cessation, to peace, to super-knowledge, to enlightenment, to Nibbāna, but only to birth in the Brahmā-world, whereas my holy life leads unfailingly to disenchantment, to dispassion, to cessation, to peace, to super-knowledge, to enlightenment, to Nibbāna. That is the Noble Eightfold Path, namely Right View, Right Thought, Right Speech, Right Action, Right Livelihood, Right Effort, Right Mindfulness, Right Concentration.'

"And, Pañcasikha, those of my disciples who have fully mastered my teaching have by their own super-knowledge realized, by the destruction of the taints in this very life, the untainted freedom of heart and mind. And of those who have not fully mastered it, some by the destruction of the five lower fetters will be reborn spontaneously, attaining thence to Nibbāna without returning to this world; some by the destruction of three fetters and the reduction of greed [lust], hatred and delusion will become Once-Returners, who will return once more to this world before making an end of suffering; and some by the destruction of three fetters will become Stream-Winners [Stream-Enterers], incapable of falling into states of woe, assured of enlightenment. Thus the going-forth of all these people was not fruitless or barren, but productive of fruit and profit.' Thus, the Lord spoke, and Pañcasikha of the Gandhabbas was delighted and rejoiced at the Lord's words. And, having saluted him, he passed him by on the right and vanished from the spot."[257]

After the Buddha attained enlightenment, he taught the Noble Eightfold Path in the Setting in Motion the Wheel of the Dhamma [the Dhammacakkappavattana Sutta]. This was the Buddha's first discourse. The Noble Eightfold Path is unique to Buddhism and is mentioned in the Mahāli Sutta: About Mahāli,[258] the Kassapa-Sīcanāda Sutta: The Great Lion's Roar,[259] the Payasi Sutta: About Payasi,[260] and also in many places in the Nikāyas. Right before his passing, the Buddha gave his final teaching to his student Subhadda. In it he said, "Now, Subhadda, in this Dhamma and discipline the Noble Eightfold Path is found, and in it are to be found ascetics of the first, second, third and fourth grade."[261] This was the last discourse of the Buddha.

---

257 D19:61–62.
258 D6:14.
259 D8:13.
260 D23:31.
261 D16:5.27.

— Appendix III —
Dependent Origination

DEPENDENT ORIGINATION IS A BUDDHIST TEACHING THAT SPEAKS to the origin and cessation of suffering. In the Early Buddhist Suttas, dependent origination refers only to the origin [anuloma, forward order] and cessation [paṭiloma, reverse order] of suffering. Phenomena's other interrelations or interdependence [conditional relations] are not referred to as dependent origination but are called paccaya, or more specifically, paṭṭhāna, in the Abhidhamma.

In the Early Buddhist Suttas, the 12 links of dependent origination appear without exception in the following standardized format:

> "With ignorance as condition, volitional [kamma] formations [come to be]; with volitional [kamma] formations as condition, consciousness; with consciousness as condition, name-and-form;[1] with name-and-form as condition, the six sense bases; with the six sense bases as condition, contact; with contact as condition, feeling; with feeling as condition, craving; with craving as condition, clinging; with clinging as condition, becoming; with becoming as condition, birth; with birth as condition, aging-and-death, sorrow, lamentation, pain, displeasure, and despair come to be. Such is the origin of this whole mass of suffering.

---

1 Name and form [nāma-rūpa] refer to mind and body.

"But with the remainderless fading away and cessation of ignorance comes cessation of volitional [kamma] formations; with
the cessation of volitional [kamma] formations, cessation of
consciousness; with the cessation of consciousness, cessation
of name-and-form; with the cessation of name-and-form,
cessation of the six sense bases; with the cessation of the six
sense bases, cessation of contact; with the cessation of contact,
cessation of feeling; with the cessation of feeling, cessation of
craving; with the cessation of craving, cessation of clinging;
with the cessation of clinging, cessation of becoming; with
the cessation of becoming, cessation of birth; with the cessation of birth, aging-and-death, sorrow, lamentation, pain,
displeasure, and despair cease. Such is the cessation of this
whole mass of suffering."[2]

In other words, only the 12 links from ignorance, volitional
[kamma] formations to birth, and aging-and-death, or the condensed versions of the 11, ten, nine ... two links of dependent
origination are called dependent origination. Thus, dependent
origination, the 12 links of dependent origination – from ignorance to aging-and-death – explain the origin and cessation of
suffering. This agrees with the truths of Buddhism – the Four
Noble Truths.[3] Knowing this, one cannot emphasize enough the
difference between dependent origination and interdependence
[conditional relations].

It is both the Southern Abhidhamma's and the Northern
Abhidharma's established theory that the teaching of the 12 links
of dependent origination explains the origin and cessation of
suffering over three lifetimes. In the Southern Abhidhamma
and the Northern Abhidharma teaching, links – 1) ignorance,
2) volitional [kamma] formations, 8) craving, 9) clinging, and

---

2 S12:1, the Dependent Origination Discourse.
3 The suffering, the origin of suffering, the cessation of suffering, and the way
leading to the cessation of suffering.

10) becoming – are understood as the cause of suffering in both the past and present life [two sets of causes]. Links – 3) consciousness, 4) name-and-form, 5) six sense bases, 6) contact, 7) feeling, 11) birth, and 12) aging-and-death – are understood as the effect of suffering in both the present and future life [two sets of effects]. The teaching also says that cause and effect repeat twice [cause-effect-cause-effect] over three lifetimes. This is why it is called "the twofold causality spanning over three lifetimes." The reason why the 12 links of dependent origination must be seen as an explanation of the cycle of rebirth over three lifetimes pertains to links 3) consciousness and 11) birth. In the Early Buddhist discourses, the Buddha said, "Ānanda, if consciousness were not to come into the mother's womb, would mind and body develop there?"[4] The commentaries consistently explain that link 3) consciousness of the 12 links of dependent origination is the rebirth-consciousness [paṭisandhivinnāṇa] or the first consciousness of one lifetime. Also, link 11) birth [jāti] is used only when meaning being born into one lifetime. Therefore, links 1) ignorance, 2) volitional [kamma] formations are of the past life, 3) consciousness, 4) name-and-form, 5) six sense bases, 6) contact, 7) feeling, 8) craving, 9) clinging, and 10) becoming concern the present life. Links 11) birth and 12) aging-and-death concern the future life.

In other discourses, especially in the Wise Man and the Fool Discourse of the Saṁyutta Nikāya,[5] dependent origination is explained as occurring over three lifetimes.[6] The Wise Man and the Fool Discourse is a very important discourse that provides the first clue to this traditional opinion. This discourse interprets the 12 links of dependent origination as "the twofold causality spanning over three lifetimes," based on four groups and 20 modes of the 12 links of dependent origination.

---

4 D15.
5 S12:19.
6 Ps.i.51–52; Vis.XVII.288–298.

In Yogācāra of Mahāyāna Buddhism, links 11) birth and 12) aging-and-death refer only to the next life; thus, the 12 links of dependent origination are known to occur over two lifetimes in this teaching. Nevertheless, in Early Buddhism and Yogācāra, the 12 links of dependent origination are accepted as a basis for understanding the origin and cessation of suffering. Most importantly, the 12 links of dependent origination show the repeated continuation of cause and effect. If this fact is overlooked, the teaching of the 12 links of dependent origination becomes very confusing.

Let's review this once more: Among the 12 links of dependent origination, links – 1) ignorance, 2) volitional [kamma] formations, 8) craving, 9) clinging, and 10) becoming – are the links of the causes of suffering; the remaining links – 3) consciousness, 4) name-and-form, 5) six sense bases, 6) contact, 7) feeling, 11) birth, and 12) aging-and-death – are the effects of suffering. The 12 links of dependent origination show the layered structures of the origin and cessation of suffering through repeated connections of the links. Therefore, it is called "the twofold causality spanning over three lifetimes."

That said, is ignorance a cause purely associated with the past life and craving a cause only associated with the present life? Certainly not! In the Path of Purification, these five components are explained to be associated with the past life or the present life: 1) ignorance, 2) volitional [kamma] formations, 8) craving, 9) clinging, and 10) becoming.[7] However, ignorance and volitional [kamma] formations are more commonly associated with past life; craving, clinging, and becoming are more often associated with the present life.

The 12 links of dependent origination have been explained in many different ways by masters of the various schools of Buddhism. According to the Abhidharma Storehouse Treatise

---

7 Vis.XVII.291.

[Abhidharmakośa-bhāṣya], the representative literature of the Northern Abhidharma, the teaching of dependent origination is interpreted using the following four theories:

1. The 12 links arise all at the same time in each moment. This is called momentary [ksanika] dependent origination.
2. The 12 links occur in succession – one at a time – in 12 consecutive moments. This is called serial [sambandhika] dependent origination.
3. The 12 links arise over three lifetimes. This is called prolonged [prakarsika] dependent origination.
4. The 12 links involve the five aggregates over 12 moments; this is called static [avasthika] dependent origination.[8]

The Abhidharma Storehouse Treatise conveys that in sūtras, only sentient beings can realize deliverance·Nibbāna by cutting off all taints; however, in the Abhidharma, dependent origination is also used to show a phenomena's conditional relationships; therefore, it applies to sentient and non-sentient beings. This theory is also explored in the Mahavibhasam, where "static" and "prolonged" dependent origination apply to sentient beings and "momentary" and "serial" dependent origination apply to non-sentient beings.

When one comes across the 12 links of dependent origination along with various teaching of dependent origination, one must keep in mind the important fact that dependent origination is a powerful tool that can be used to reveal the non-self. The teaching of dependent origination begs us to relinquish ideas of a self, true-self, great-self, master, etc. An attempt to sublimate the teaching of dependent origination [the origin and cessation of suffering] as the "interdependence [paṭṭhāna] of all conditioned phenomena – the 24 modes of conditionality [paccaya]" – is to

---

8 According to the Abhidharma Storehouse Treatise, Sarvāstivāda subscribed only to static dependent origination.

clearly establish the theoretical basis for the non-self of all conditioned phenomena.

To eliminate suffering, do all 12 links of dependent origination need to be eliminated? I do not believe they do. Perhaps just one link needs to be eliminated. If one sees dependent origination as links of cause and effect, only the causal links associated with specific suffering must be eliminated. The central point of the causal links of suffering is craving. The Four Noble Truths list craving as the cause of all suffering and define the absence of craving as Nibbāna.

So, how can we eliminate craving? We must practice the 37 requisites of enlightenment, represented as the Noble Eightfold Path.

What is clinging and craving? With craving as a condition, cause, and foundation, clinging comes to be. With the cessation of craving, clinging ceases. With such knowledge, one understands clinging, its origin, and how to eliminate it. One who intensifies craving, intensifies clinging. One who intensifies clinging, intensifies suffering. One who intensifies suffering, becomes subject to birth, aging, illness, death, sorrow, lamentation, pain, displeasure, and despair.

Four kinds of clinging:

"Clinging to sensual pleasures,
clinging to views,
clinging to rules and observances,
clinging to a doctrine of self."[9]

Three kinds of craving:

"Craving for sensual pleasures,
craving for existence,
craving for extermination."[10]

---

9 M11:9.
10 S56:11.

— Appendix IV—
Charts

· Establishment and History of Early Buddhism and Pāli Suttas
· Theory of Early Buddhism
· Practice of Early Buddhism: the 37 Requisites of Enlightenment
· The Core Teaching of Early Buddhism: the Four Noble Truths and the Noble Eightfold Path
· The 12 Links of Dependent Origination: the Origin and Cessation of Suffering
· The 12 Links of Dependent Origination and the Ten Fetters
· The Five Aggregates
· The Four Groups and 82 Dhammas of Theravāda Buddhism
· 52 Types of Mental Factors
· 28 Types of Materiality
· Seven Stages of Purification and Knowledge of Vipassanā

Establishment and History
of Early Buddhism and Pāli Suttas

Sutta	Contents	Structure
Dīgha Nikāya	The Long Discourses of the Buddha	Three Divisions, 34 Suttas
Majjhima Nikāya	The Middle Length Discourses of the Buddha	15 Divisions 152 Suttas
Saṁyutta Nikāya	The Connected Discourses of the Buddha	Five Sections, 56 Chapters, 2889 Suttas
Aṅguttara Nikāya	The Numerical Discourses of the Buddha	11 Books
Khuddaka Nikāya	The Collection of Little Texts	15 Books

Council	Background	Time Period
First Council	Soon after the Buddha's passing, 500 Arahants chanted together Dhamma for seven months. The Collection of Discourses was memorized by the Ven. Ānanda and the Rules of Conduct were recited by the Ven. Upāli. Both collections were compiled at the First Buddhist Council.	Two months[1] after the Buddha's passing.

---

1 According to the preface of the Dīgha Nikāya Aṭṭhakathā, the Buddha's PariNibbāna was on April 15th [lunar calendar]. For the next two months, following events took place: seven days of viewing [funeral visitation], cremation over seven days, seven days of prayers over sarira [sacred relics], sarira were divided 21 days later on May 5th [lunar calendar], the First Council commenced on June 15th [lunar calendar]. §18(DA.i.6), §69(DA.i.25)

Council	Background	Time Period
Second Council	The Second Council was held in Vaisali and attended by 700 high-level monks. The key issue of this Council was about certain infringement of rules [dispute over the ten Points]. Sthaviravāda/ Theravāda were against the Ten Points, and Mahāsāṃghika or the Great Community were for the ten Points.	100 years after the Buddha's passing.
Third Council	The Third Council was convened in Kumanahar near Patna in 235 B.C.E. for nine months, attended by 1,000 high-level monks. The traditional recitation of the Sutta and the Vinaya by the monks occurred. Abhidhamma of Theravāda Buddhism is supposedly completed at the Third Council.	Emperor Ashoka was crowned in the 218 years after the Buddha's Parinibbāna. The Third Council was called in 17 years of the Emperor's reign. [235 B.C.E.]
Fourth Council	The Fourth Council was held in Sri Lanka under the patronage of King Vattagamani. The Theravadin Pāli Canon [Tipiṭaka] was committed to writing for the first time in Sinhalese.	The First Century B.C.E.

Theory of Early Buddhism

The Five Aggregates	Material Form, Feeling, Perception, Mental Formations, and Consciousness.
The 12 Sense Bases	Eye, Ear, Nose, Tongue, Body, Mind, Visible Forms, Sound, Odor, Taste, Tactile Objects, and Mental Objects.
The 18 Elements	Eye element, visible form element, eye-consciousness element. Ear element, sound element, ear-consciousness element. Nose element, odor element, nose-consciousness element. Tongue element, taste element, tongue-consciousness element. Body element, tactile-object element, body-consciousness element. Mind element, mental-object element, mind-consciousness element.
The 22 Faculties of Human Beings	Eye, Ear, Nose, Tongue, Body, Mind, Femininity, Masculinity, Life, Bodily pleasure, Bodily pain, Mental joy, Mental grief, Equanimity, Faith, Energy, Mindfulness, Concentration, Understanding [Wisdom], I shall-come-to-know-the-unknown, Final-knowledge, and Final knower.
The Four Noble Truth	The Noble Truth of Suffering. The Noble Truth of the Origin of Suffering. The Noble Truth of the Cessation of Suffering. The Noble Truth of the Way Leading to the Cessation of Suffering.
The 12 Links of Dependent Origination	Ignorance, Volitional [kamma] formations, Consciousness, Name-and-form, the Six sense bases, Feeling, Craving, Clinging, Becoming, Birth, Aging-and-death, Sorrow, Lamentation, Pain, Displeasure, and Despair.

Practice of Early Buddhism: the 37 Requisites of Enlightenment

The Four Foundations of Mindfulness	The Subjects of Mindfulness: Body, Feeling, Mind, and Mental Objects.
The Four Right Efforts	Striving for the non-arising of unarisen unwholesome dhammas, Striving for the abandonment of arisen unwholesome dhammas, Striving for the arising of unarisen wholesome dhammas, Striving for the development of arisen wholesome dhammas.
The Four Bases for Spiritual Power	Desire, Energy, Mind, and Investigation.
The Five Faculties	The Faculty of Faith, Energy, Mindfulness, Concentration, and Wisdom.
The Five Powers	The Power of Faith, Energy, Mindfulness, Concentration, and Wisdom.
The Seven Factors of Enlightenment	Mindfulness, Investigation, Energy, Rapture, Tranquility, Concentration, and Equanimity.
The Noble Eightfold Path	Right View, Right Intention, Right Speech, Right Action, Right Livelihood, Right Effort, Right Mindfulness, and Right Concentration.

The Core Teaching of Early Buddhism: the Four Noble Truths and the Noble Eightfold Path

The Four Noble Truths
The Noble Truth of Suffering [dukkha ariya-sacca].
The Noble Truth of the Origin of Suffering [dukkha-samudaya ariya-sacca].
The Noble Truth of the Cessation of Suffering [dukkha-nirodha ariya-sacca].
The Noble Truth of the Way Leading to the Cessation of Suffering [dukkha-nirodha-gāmini-paṭipadā ariya-sacca].

The Noble Eightfold Path			
Wisdom	The Right View	sammā-diṭṭhi	Knowing the Four Noble Truths and the 12 Links of Dependent Origination.
Wisdom	The Right Intention	sammā-saṅkappa	Intention of renunciation. Intention of non-ill will. Intention of harmlessness.
Morality	The Right Speech	sammā-vācā	Abstinence from false speech, divisive speech, harsh speech, and idle chatter.
Morality	The Right Action	sammā-kammanta	Abstinence from destruction of life, taking what is not given, and sexual misconduct.

The Noble Eightfold Path			
Morality	The Right Livelihood	sammā-ājīva	Having abandoned a wrong mode of livelihood, earns his living by right livelihood. The monastics must make a living receiving alms and observing non-possession. Very importantly, monastics should not engage in fortune-telling and divination. Lay Buddhists must make a living by engaging in a proper occupation or trade. Lay Buddhists should not be engaged in trading in weapons, trading in living beings, trading in meat, trading in intoxicants, and trading in poisons.
Concentration	The Right Efforts	sammā-vāyāma	Striving for the non-arising of unarisen unwholesome dhammas, Striving for the abandonment of arisen unwholesome dhammas, Striving for the arising of unarisen wholesome dhammas, Striving for the development of arisen wholesome dhammas.
Concentration	The Right Mindfulness	sammā-sati	Being mindful of the body, feeling, mind, and mental objects.

225

The Noble Eightfold Path			
Concentration	The Right Concentration	sammā-samādhi	Entering and dwelling in the first, second, third, and fourth jhāna. Having overcome the five hindrances [sensual desire, ill will, sloth and torpor, restlessness and remorse, and doubt] and by practicing the right concentration, one attains the four jhānas, progressively experiencing the rapture-happiness-tranquility-equanimity.

The 12 Links of Dependent Origination: the Origin and Cessation of Suffering

Three Lives	12 Links	20 Modes and 4 Groups
Past	1. Ignorance 2. Volitional [kamma] Formations	Five causes of the past – 1, 2, 8, 9, 10
Present	3. Consciousness 4. Name-and-form 5. Six sense bases 6. Contact 7. Feeling	Five resultants of the present – 3, 4, 5, 6, 7
	8. Craving 9. Clinging 10. Becoming	Five causes of the present – 8, 9, 10, 1, 2
Future	11. Birth [as rebirth] 12. Aging-and-death	Five resultants of the future – 3, 4, 5, 6, 7

THREE CONNECTIONS:
1. The cause of the past and the resultant of the present. [Between #2 volitional, kamma formations and #3 consciousness.]
2. The resultant of the present and the cause of the present. [Between #7 feeling and #8 craving.]
3. The cause of the present and the resultant of the future. [Between #10 becoming and #11 birth, as rebirth.]

THREE ROUNDS:
1. The rounds of the defilements. [#1 ignorance, #8 craving, #9 clinging.]
2. The rounds of the kamma. [#2 volitional, kamma formations, #10 a portion of becoming.]
3. The rounds of the retribution. [#3 consciousness through #7 feeling, #10 a portion of becoming, #11 birth, as rebirth, #12 aging-end-death.]

TWO CAUSES:
1. Ignorance: the past to present. Craving: the present to future.

The 12 Links of Dependent Origination and the Ten Fetters

12 Links of Dependent Origination [Paticca-samuppada]		
12	Aging-and-Death	Jarāmaraṇa
11	Birth	Jāti
10	Existence	Bhava
9	Clinging	Upādāna
8	Craving	Taṇhā
7	Feeling	Vedanā
6	Contact	Phassa
5	Six Sense Bases	Saḷāyatana
4	Name-and-Form	Nāmarūpa
3	Consciousness	Viññāna
2	Volitional [kamma] Formations	Saṅkhāra
1	Ignorance	Avijjā

Ten Fetters [Saṁyojana]				
Arahant	10	Ignorance	avijjā	Higher fetter
Arahant	9	Restlessness	uddhacca	Higher fetter
Arahant	8	Conceit or self-measurement.	māna	Higher fetter
Arahant	7	Attachment to the formless spheres.	arūpa-rāga	Higher fetter
Arahant	6	Attachment to the form spheres.	rūpa-rāga	Higher fetter
Anāgamin	5	Ill Will	byāpādo	Lower fetter
Sakadāgamin	4	Sensual lust	kāma-rāga	Lower fetter
Sotāpanna	3	Doubt	vicikicchā	Lower fetter
Sotāpanna	2	Attachment to moral precepts and religious ritual.	sīlabbata-parāmāsa	Lower fetter
Sotāpanna	1	Self-view	sakkāya-diṭṭhi	Lower fetter

The stream-enterer is a noble one who has abandoned the three fetters of self-view, attachment to rules and ritual, doubt; the once-returner is a noble one who has not only abandoned the previous three fetters but also weakened the two fetters of sensual lust and ill will. The non-returner is a noble one who has completely abandoned the lower five fetters; the Arahant is a noble one who has abandoned all ten fetters.

GREAT STRIVING
Striving for the arising of the Five Powers,
Striving for the non-arising of the Five Hindrances.

THE FIVE POWERS
Faith: Confidence in the Buddha, Dhamma, Saṅgha, Morality.
Energy: Four Right Strivings.
Mindfulness: Four Foundations of Mindfulness.
Concentration: Four Jhānas.
Wisdom: Four Noble Truths.

THE FIVE HINDRANCES
Sensual Desire.
Ill Will.
Sloth and Torpor.
Restlessness and Remorse.
Doubt.

The Five Aggregates

Five Aggregates: Panca-khandha			
Material form, matter, materiality: Rūpa	Name, mentality: Nāma		
	Mental factors, mental, Mental concomitants: Cetasikā		Mind, cognizance, consciousness: Citta.
	Feeling: Vedanā	Perception: Sannā	Mental Formations: Saṅkhārā.	Consciousness: Vinnāṇa.

The Four Groups and 82 Dhammas
of Theravāda Buddhism

All Phenomena: Sabbe dhammā			
Conditioned Phenomena: Saṅkhara-dhammā			Unconditioned Phenomenon: Asaṅkhāra-dhamma.
I. Mind, cognizance, consciousness: Citta	II. Mental factors, mental, mental concomitants: Cetasikā	III. Material form, matter, materiality: Rūpa	IV. Extinction of lust, hatred, and delusion: Nibbāna.
One type	52 types 1. Mental factors that become common with others [13 types]. 2. Unwholesome mental factors [14 types]. 3. Beautiful mental factors [25 types].	28 types 1. Produced materiality: Nipphanna-rūpa [18 types]. 2. Unproduced materiality: Anipphanna-rūpa [ten types]. *Excluding the ten unproduced materiality, the 72 types are the ultimate realities: paramattha-dhamma.	One type
Consciousness: Vinnāṇa	Feeling: Vedanā. Perception: Sannā. Mental Formations: Saṅkhārā.	Material form, matter, materiality: Rūpa.	

231

52 Types of Mental Factors

MENTAL FACTORS THAT BECOME COMMON WITH OTHERS:
[ANNA SAMĀNA]

*These 13 become moral or immoral according to the type of consciousness in which they occur.

SEVEN *UNIVERSAL* MENTAL FACTORS
1. Contact: Phassa
2. Feeling: Vedanā
3. Perception: Sannā
4. Volition: Cetanā
5. One-pointedness: Ekaggatā
6. Life faculty: Jīvitindriya
7. Attention: Manasikāra

SIX *OCCASIONAL* MENTAL FACTORS
8. Applied thought: Vitakka
9. Sustained thought: Vicāra
10. Determination: Adhimokkha
11. Energy: Viriya
12. Rapture: Pīti
13. Desire [to act]: Chanda

UNWHOLESOME MENTAL FACTORS:
[AKUSALA-CETASIKĀ]
FOUR *UNIVERSAL* UNWHOLESOME MENTAL FACTORS
14. Delusion: Moha
15. Lack of shame: Ahirika
16. Disregard for consequence: Anottappa
17. Restlessness: Uddhacca

TEN *OCCASIONAL* UNWHOLESOME MENTAL FACTORS
THREE MENTAL FACTORS OF THE LUST-GROUP

18. Lust: Lobha
19. Wrong View: Diṭṭhi
20. Conceit: Māna

FOUR MENTAL FACTORS OF THE HATRED-GROUP

21. Hatred: Dosa
22. Envy: Issā
23. Miserliness: Macchariya
24. Remorse: Kukkucca

CONSCIOUSNESS: CITTA UJUKATĀ
TWO MENTAL FACTORS CONNECTED TO SLOTH.

25. Sloth: Thīna
26. Torpor: Middha

ONE MENTAL FACTOR CONNECTED TO DOUBT.

27. Doubt: Vicikicchā

BEAUTIFUL MENTAL FACTORS:
[SOBHANA-CETASIKĀ]
***19 UNIVERSAL* MENTAL FACTORS**

28. Faith: Saddhā
29. Mindfulness: Sati
30. Moral shame: Hirī
31. Regard for consequence: Ottappa
32. Non-lust: Alobha
33. Non-hatred: Adosa
34. Equanimity: Tatramajjhattatā
35. Tranquility of mental body: Kāya passaddhi
36. Tranquility of consciousness: Citta passaddhi
37. Lightness of mental body: Kāya lahutā
38. Lightness of consciousness: Citta lahutā
39. Pliancy of mental body: Kāya mudutā

40. Pliancy of consciousness: Citta mudutā
41. Wieldiness of mental body: Kāya kammannatā
42. Wieldiness of consciousness: Citta kammannatā
43. Proficiency of mental body: Kāya pāgunnatā
44. Proficiency of consciousness: Citta pāgunnatā
45. Rectitude of mental body: Kāya ujukatā
46. Rectitude of consciousness: Citta lahutā

SIX *UNIVERSAL* MENTAL FACTORS
THREE ABSTINENCES: VIRATI

47. Right speech: Sammā vācā
48. Right action: Sammā kammanta
49. Right livelihood: Sammā ājīva

TWO IMMEASURABLE: APPAMANNA

50. Compassion: Karuṇā
51. Sympathetic joy: Muditā

NON-DELUSION: AMOHA

52. Faculty of wisdom: Pannindriya

28 Types of Materiality

Produced materiality: Nipphanna-rūpa [18 types]	Basic elements: Bhūta-rūpa	1	Earth element: Paṭhavī-dhātu	Basic elements: Bhūta-rūpa [4 types]
		2	Water element: Āpo-dhātu	
		3	Fire element: Tejo-dhātu	
		4	Wind element: Vāyo-dhātu	
	Sensitivity materiality: Pasāda-rūpa	5	Eye sensitivity: Cakkhu-pasāda	Derived materiality: Upādāya-rūpa [24 types]
		6	Ear sensitivity: Sota-pasāda	
		7	Nose sensitivity: Ghāna-pasāda	
		8	Tongue sensitivity: Jivhā-pasāda	
		9	Body sensitivity: Kāya-pasāda	
	Objective materiality: Gacara-rūpa	10	Visible form: Rūpa	
		11	Sound: Sadda	
		12	Odor: Gandha	
		13	Taste or flavor: Rasa	
			*Since tangible is not an element of its own, but is an element of earth, fire, and wind of the four great elements, it is excluded from the objective materiality.	
	Sex materiality: Bhāva-rūpa	14	Female sex-materiality: Itthībhāva or itthaīa	
		15	Male sex-materiality: Pumbhāva or purisatta	
	Heart materiality: Hadaya-rūpa	16	Heart-basis: Hadaya-vatthu	
	Life materiality: Jīvita-rūpa	17	Life faculty: Jīvitindriya	
	Nutriment materiality: Āhāra-rūpa	18	Nutritive essence: Ojā	
Unproduced materiality: Anipphanna-rūpa [Ten types]	Delimitation materiality: Pariccheda-rūpa	19	Space element: Ākāsa-dhātu	
	Intimation materiality: Viññatti-rūpa	20	Bodily intimation: Kāya-viññatti	
		21	Verbal intimation: Vacī-viññatti	
	Alteration materiality: Vikāra-rūpa	22	Lightness of materiality: Rūpassa lahutā	
		23	Malleability of materiality: Rūpassa mudutā	
		24	Wieldiness of materiality: Rūpassa kammaññatā	
	Characteristic materiality: Lakkhaṇa-rūpa	25	Growth of materiality: Upacaya	
		26	Continuity of materiality: Santati	
		27	Aging of materiality: Jaratā	
		28	Impermanence of materiality: Aniccatā	

28 Types of Materiality [Rūpa]

235

Seven Stages of Purification and Knowledge of Vipassanā

Seven Purifications	Knowledge of Vipassanā
1. Purification of morality.	The fourfold purity of morality.
2. Purification of mind.	The access-concentration and absorption-concentration.
3. Purification of view.	The insight of the characteristics of mentality-materiality.
4. Purification by overcoming doubt.	The knowledge of clearly knowing the cause and condition of mentality-materiality.
5. Purification by knowledge and vision of what is path and not path.	1. The knowledge of meditation. 2. The knowledge of arising and passing away [weak stage].
6. Purification by knowledge and vision of the way.	2. The knowledge of arising and passing away [mature stage]. 3. The knowledge of dissolution. 4. The knowledge of terror. 5. The knowledge of danger. 6. The knowledge of disgust. 7. The knowledge of desire for deliverance. 8. The knowledge of re-observation. 9. The knowledge of equanimity about formations. 10. The knowledge in conformity.
	The change-of-lineage knowledge. [This does not belong to the purification.]
7. Purification by knowledge and vision	The knowledge of the path. The knowledge of the fruit. The knowledge of retrospection.

— Appendix V—
The True Nature of the Five Aggregates, the Four Noble Truths, Torrents of Clinging

THE IMPERMANENT SUTTA

[BUDDHA] "Bhikkhus, form is impermanent, feeling is impermanent, perception is impermanent, volitional [mental] formations are impermanent, consciousness is impermanent. Seeing thus, bhikkhus, the instructed noble disciple experiences revulsion toward form, revulsion toward feeling, revulsion toward perception, revulsion toward volitional [mental] formations, revulsion toward consciousness. Experiencing revulsion, he becomes dispassionate. Through dispassion [his mind] is liberated. When it is liberated there comes the knowledge: 'It's liberated.' He understands: 'Destroyed is birth, the holy life has been lived, what had to be done has been done, there is no more for this state of being.'"[1]

THE STREAM-ENTERER SUTTA

[BUDDHA] At Sāvatthī. "Bhikkhus, there are these five aggregates subject to clinging. What five? The form aggregate subject to clinging, the feeling aggregate subject to clinging, the perception aggregate subject to clinging, mental formations

---

1 S22:12.

subject to clinging, the consciousness aggregate subject to clinging.

"When, bhikkhus, a noble disciple understands as they really are the origin and the passing away, the gratification, the danger, and the escape in the case of these five aggregates subject to clinging, then he is called a noble disciple who is a stream-enterer, no longer bound to the nether world, fixed in destiny, with enlightenment as his destination."[2]

THE VAJIRĀ SUTTA

[MĀRA] "By whom has this being been created? Where is the maker of the being? Where has the being arisen? Where does the being cease?"

[BHIKKHUNI VAJIRĀ] "Why now do you assume 'a being'? Māra, is that your speculative view? This is a heap of sheer formations: Here no being is found. Just as, with an assemblage of parts, the word 'chariot' is used, So, when the aggregates exist, there is the convention 'a being.' It's only suffering that comes to be, suffering that stands and falls away. Nothing but suffering comes to be, nothing but suffering ceases."[3]

THE FLOODS SUTTA

[BUDDHA] "Bhikkhus, there are these four floods. What four? The flood of sensuality, the flood of existence, the flood of views, the flood of ignorance.

"Bhikkhus, the four right efforts are to be developed for direct knowledge of these four floods, for the full understanding of them, for their utter destruction, for their abandoning.

---

2 S22:109.
3 S5:10.

"Bhikkhus, there are these four right efforts. What four? Here, bhikkhus, a bhikkhu generates desire for the non-arising of unarisen evil unwholesome states; he makes an effort, arouses energy, applies his mind, and strives. He generates desire for the abandoning of arisen evil unwholesome states; he makes an effort, arouses energy, applies his mind, and strives. He generates desire for the arising of unarisen wholesome states; he makes an effort, arouses energy, applies his mind, and strives. He generates desire for the maintenance of arisen wholesome states, for their nondecay, increase, expansion, and fulfillment by development; he makes an effort, arouses energy, applies his mind, and strives."[4]

THE SACCA-SAṀYUTTA

The Four Noble Truths are the basic subject of the Saccasaṁyutta Discourse [the Connected Discourses on the Truths], the great finale of the Saṁyutta Nikāya, which is a collection of the Buddha's teaching organized by subject matter. The Saccasaṁyutta Discourse, which includes 131 discourses, emphasizes that the reason for developing concentration[5] and becoming a monastic[6] is to penetrate the Four Noble Truths. Furthermore, this discourse states that when one reflects and speaks, one should always reflect and speak about the Four Noble Truths.[7] "It is because he has fully awakened to these Four Noble Truths as they really are that the Tathāgata is

---

4 S49:45–54.
5 S56:1.
6 S56:3–4.
7 S58:8.

called the Arahant, the Perfectly Enlightened One."[8] It is also emphasized, "The destruction of the taints comes about for one who knows and sees."[9]

8 S56:23.
9 S56:25.

Epilogue

KNOWING THE DHAMMA MEANS KNOWING THE FOUR NOBLE Truths; knowing the Four Noble Truths means knowing who and what I am and am not; knowing "I" means knowing the truth of the birth-aging-illness-death cycle and how to escape from it.

I learned that I would die someday when I was a third-grade student, about nine years old. One late autumn evening, my father and I sat together after dinner. Interestingly, what my father told me that evening determined my direction in life. Because of that conversation, I am here today.

Before Korea was liberated from Japanese occupation and before I was born, my father and my brother-in-law had a small maritime business. They delivered merchandises to merchants around the coastal water region with a small cargo ship. The story my father told me that evening starts from an incident in which he was involved with that company.

My father and my brother-in-law were delivering merchandises from Ulsan, port Bang-eojin to the port of Busan. While sailing to the port of Busan, two shippers who chartered the ship suddenly pirated the vessel. My father and brother-in-law got into a fistfight with these two, and all four of them fell into the sea. Miraculously, my father and brother-in-law survived.

My brother-in-law was injured with a gunshot wound to the jaw and my father, despite his maritime business, did not know how to swim. So, how did they survive in the ocean? According to the words of my father, "Without anyone's help!" My father

believed that their survival was indeed a miracle, which he cred-
ited to the merit he accrued from his life-long chanting of the
Avalokiteśvara bodhisattva and my brother-in-law's good character. One pirate died in the ocean; the other was turned over to
the police. The police record showed that these two men tried to
seize the ship and illegally enter Japan.

After telling me this story, my father abruptly changed the
subject and told me that any being born is bound to die. He said,
"Hwan, because you are born, you too will die someday. You must
not forget this fact."

As a nine-year boy who learned for the first time that he would
eventually die, I was shocked and disoriented for a while. It was
as if I had been hit on the back of my head with a hammer! Just
retelling this story – half a century later – brings back to me that
same fear that I felt then. My father called my name quietly and
said, "Whatever kind of work you do in the future, do not neglect
your study of Buddhism."

The words of my father that day have guided the direction
of my life. Although my understanding of Buddhism continues
to grow, I strive daily to live by the Buddha's teaching. Through
this stumbling journey following the Buddha's teaching, I came
to know a few things: I was born a human being, I encountered
Buddhism, and although a bit late, I finally encountered Early
Buddhism, about which I have absolute confidence and feel
infinite gratitude and joy.

For those who are interested in studying Buddhism, I would
like to share what I have learned. First, studying Buddhism starts
with a clear recognition of the existential fact of suffering in life.
In other words, one must fully understand the Noble Truth of
Suffering. Only then one will develop faith. Meaningful Buddhist
study begins when one faces the truth of suffering.

Next, I have found that anyone who wants to walk this path
must simplify his or her life. A person on this path cannot be too
busy; this is essential. It is also imperative that one does not have

close relations with unwise people because the Buddha said that who you become is dependent on those you associate with.

The entirety of the theory and practice of Buddhism are distilled in the Four Noble Truths. So, as we engage in any task, anywhere, the Four Noble Truths must be our compass. The priority tasks must be those that lead us from ignorance to enlightenment. We must make an ironclad commitment to avoid tasks that do not lead us to enlightenment. Only then shall we become unshakably confident, regardless of life's difficulties.

As I look back on my life, I am relieved that I have time to meditate quietly. Of course, this is possible due to the many important relationships I have had over the course of my life. I want to express my gratitude to those who helped me along the way. First of all, I would like to thank my parents for bringing me into this world, raising me, and guiding me to Buddhism. I also would like to recognize and thank Bhikkhu Kyung-Bong of Tongdosa Temple, Gukrak Hermitage, Lee, Ki Young, Ph.D. [1922–1996], Shu, Kyung Su, Ph.D. [1925–1986], Prof. Jung, Byung Jo of Dongguk University, my great teacher, Kim, Sha Chul, Ph.D., U Jotika Sayadaw who taught a ten-day meditation retreat at Shimwoo Sanbang located in Gyeongju, Namsan, Bhikkhuni Daerim, the head of the Center for Early Buddhist Studies, and Bhikkhu Kakmuk, instructor of the Center for Early Buddhist Studies. Whenever I have difficulty with government administrative issues in running my business, Jung, Mun Hwa [former Mayor of Busan who served as a member of the National Assembly, 15th and 16th] smiled and did his best to solve the problem. And finally, I cannot give enough thanks to my partner, Choi, Eun Young who continues to cheer me on to keep up with my study.

There are intangible things that I am grateful for as well. I am actually thankful for the extreme poverty I experienced throughout my youth and for my frail body. The poverty motivated me to become economically self-reliant. This, in turn, allowed my intellect to mature. My fragile body was a constant reminder to me that death could come at any time. That fact led me to the question, "What is the point of life?" This question drew me closer to the meaning of the Dhamma. I give thanks that these intangible things have been an important part of my life.

Finally, I would like to assert that everything I have written in this book, including interpretation and explanations, are mine alone. For them, I take full responsibility.

Blessings to all living beings! Thank you.
Fall of Year 2009
Shimwoo Sanbang, Gyeongju, Namsan
Mujin, Kyung Hwan Hwang

Bibliography

Excerpts from *The Numerical Discourses of The Buddha: A Complete Translation of the Anguttara Nikâya*, translated by Bhikkhu Bodhi. Copyright © 2012 by Bhikkhu Bodhi. Reprinted with the permission of The Permissions Company, LLC on behalf of Wisdom Publications, wisdompubs.org.

Excerpts from *The Long Discourses of the Buddha: A Translation of the Digha Nikaya*. Copyright © 1987, 1995 by Maurice Walshe. Reprinted with the permission of The Permissions Company, LLC on behalf of Wisdom Publications, wisdompubs.org.

Excerpts from *The Middle Length Discourses of The Buddha: A New Translation of the Majjhima Nikâya*, translated by Bhikkhu Ñânamoli, edited and revised by Bhikkhu Bodhi. Copyright © 1995 by Bhikkhu Bodhi. Reprinted with the permission of The Permissions Company, LLC on behalf of Wisdom Publications, wisdompubs.org.

Excerpts from *The Connected Discourses of the Buddha: A New Translation of the Samyutta Nikâya,* translated by Bhikkhu Bodhi. Copyright © 2000 by Bhikkhu Bodhi. Reprinted with the permission of The Permissions Company, LLC on behalf of Wisdom Publications, wisdompubs.org.

[Translation of the Dhammapada] Acharya Buddharakkhita, the Buddhist Publication Society (BPS), Kandy, Sri Lanka 2013.

[Translation of the Dhammapada] Gil Fronsdal, Shambhala 2006.

[Translation of the Theragāthā] Bhikkhu Sujato, Sutta Central.

[Translation of the Udāna, Nibbāna Sutta] John D. Ireland, the Buddhist Publication Society (BPS), Kandy, Sri Lanka 2012.

[Translation of the Udāna] Ṭhānissaro Bhikkhu 2012.

[Visuddhimagga: The Path of Purification] Bhikkhu Nāṇamoli, the Buddhist Publication Society (BPS), Kandy, Sri Lanka 1999, 2013.

[The Way of Mindfulness, the Satipatthana Sutta and its Commentary] Soma Thera, the Buddhist Publication Society (BPS), Kandy, Sri Lanka 2013.

[Introduction to Early Buddhism] Authored by Bhikkhu Kakmuk, Translated by Nancy Acord a.k.a. Sohn, Dong Ran, the Center for Early Buddhist Studies, Nibbāna Buddhist Education Foundation 2017.

[Understanding Early Buddhism] Authored by Bhikkhu Kakmuk, the Center for Early Buddhist Studies 2010, 2015.

[Contemplation of Feeling: The Discourse-Grouping on the Feelings] Translated from the Pali, with an Introduction by Nyanaponika Thera, the Buddhist Publication Society (BPS), Kandy, Sri Lanka 2013.

[The Heart Sūtra with Explanatory Notes] Authored by Sha Chul Kim, Ph.D. and Prof. Kyung Hwan Hwang 2009, 2012, 2016.

[Translation of History of Indian Buddhism by Etienne Lamotte, Vol. 1–2] Bhikkhu Hojin, Shi-Gong-Sha 2006.

— About the Author —
Prof. Kyung Hwan Hwang

KYUNG HWAN HWANG WAS BORN IN THE PORT OF ONSAN, THE
city of Ulsan, South Korea. He graduated from Dongguk University graduate school with a degree in Ethics Education. Since 1977
he has been active in the Korean Institute for Buddhist Studies as
a director and a research fellow. Currently, he is a senior research
fellow at the Center for Early Buddhist Studies. Since 1980 he has
been an active member of People to People International. He was
President of the Korea Center for People to People International
in 1996 and 1997.

His accomplishments include the following:

13th President of the Korea Center for People to People
International.

Director and Research Fellow of the Korean Institute for
Buddhist Studies.

CEO of the Ulsan Buddhist Broadcasting System.

Senior Research Fellow of the Center for Early Buddhist
Studies.

President of the Right Buddhist Practice Forum.

Professor of the Dongguk University Continuing Education
Center [Gyeong-ju campus].

Honorary Doctor of Philosophy from the Dongguk
University.

CEO of the Jinyang Tanker CO., LTD.

CEO of the Gyeong-ju ICS.

His publications include:

Heart Sūtra with Explanatory Notes, authored by Sa Chul
    Kim, Ph.D. and Prof. Kyung Hwan Hwang.
Research Paper – "A Study on the Ethical Nature of Silla
    Buddhism," authored by Prof. Kyung Hwan Hwang.

Translator

NANCY ACORD [A.K.A. SOHN, DONG RAN] WAS BORN IN SEOUL, Korea in 1957 and moved to the United States in 1976. After completing her bachelor's degree in business administration at California State University in Los Angeles, she worked as a Certified Public Accountant for international accounting firms and as a Chief Financial Officer and Chief Executive Officer at a US national healthcare organization. Since retiring from her business career in 2004, she has devoted herself to Buddhist studies. In 2014, she founded the Nibbāna Buddhist Education Foundation in the United States.

Editor

MARY GARCIA GRANT STARTED HER WRITING CAREER AS A TYPE-setter, proofreader, copy editor and journalist for the Emporia Gazette, the American newspaper brought to prominence by the Pulitzer Prize-winning writer William Allen White in Emporia, Kansas. Later she worked at NASA's Goddard Institute for Space Studies in New York City as an editing assistant to scientists who researched global climate change. Her primary study was in violin performance at Rice University in Houston and the City University of New York at Queens College. She has been a violinist with the Kansas City Symphony for 30 years, but still enjoys writing and editing.

Made in the USA
Columbia, SC
20 September 2022